Our Love

Story of Two Teenagers in Love

MARGARET PORTER

ISBN 978-1-64114-096-6 (paperback)
ISBN 978-1-64114-097-3 (digital)

Christian Faith Publishing, Inc.
832 Park Avenue
Meadville, PA 16335
www.christianfaithpublishing.com

Printed in the United States of America

Dedication

To my husband, Elijah Porter, with-
out you, there would not be a book;
Iona Porter Morrison, my friend for six-
ty-six years and my sister-law;
Pastor Clark Alexander, my spiritual advisor and his wife Lucina;
Marisa Triplett, my friend and advisor;
Josephine Nobile, my friend who gave me my first monetary check;
Carolyn Schugart, my friend and book publisher advisor;
Maria Coval, my friend who helped me pre-
pare my book to be published;
Elijah's family and my family along with our
friends who encouraged me every day;
Mark Porter, my son who made sure that I had a good keyboard.

Contents

Acknowledgements..7

Introduction...11

Sixty-Five Years of Love 13

Early Dates...14

    Picture: Elijah and Margaret as Teenagers 16

Margaret's Vacation 17

    First Romantic Letter to Margaret 18

    Picture of Margaret 19

Elijah's Navy Story...20

Letters and Pictures (1951)..22

Letters and Pictures (1952)..51

Letters and Pictures (1953)..99

Letters (1954)...147

Planning the Wedding (Picture) 190

Letters (1955)...191

Wedding Invitation 198

Wedding Day 199

    Wedding Pictures 200

    Elijah and Margaret's First Apartment (Picture).....209

Family...210

    Family Pictures...212

Closeness of Elijah and Margaret......................................220

Special Card to Elijah 223

Travels 224

Margaret and Elijah Porter's Golden Wedding Anniversary 227

Our Love 228

Special Pictures 230

Mother's Day Story 241

Special Awards from Church 242

Words of Congratulations 244

Sixtieth Wedding Anniversary 247

Special Pictures 247

Married for Life 260

Words of Congratulations 264

Final Thoughts (Margaret) 273

Acknowledgements

I am grateful to my parents, Claude and Pinkie Williams, for raising me to become the young girl and then grew into the woman that I became to be able to know what I would want out of life. My sister Catherine and I were raised in church. Since we lived two doors from the church, I was able to go as often as I wanted to without having my parents take me.

When my sister and I were growing up as young children, it was during World War 2. We only saw our father on Sunday afternoons as he worked almost twenty-four hours a day in the job that he had which was very involved with the war. He would go to work very early in the morning, and we would be asleep when he returned in the late hours of the night. He worked very hard to take care of his family.

Because my father worked so much, my mother was the person that disciplined my sister and me. We did not get too many beating from her, as she liked to pinch us or take away something that she thought was important to us. If we had done something that she thought we should be punished for before Sunday, she would keep us home and not let us go to Sunday school. She knew that this would hurt me more than a beating as I always enjoyed going to church.

There was a deacon at Mount Calvary Baptist Church where we attended who also had a dry cleaning business. When he would come on Monday at our house to pick up my mother's dry cleaning and we had not been to church the Sunday before, he would ask my mother why, and she would reply that we had misbehaved and had to be punished. Deacon Jimmerson would plead with my mother to please find another way to punish us. After a few times, she finally listened to him and stopped keeping us away from church.

After the war was over, we saw more of our father, and he took over our punishment. His form of punishment was beating. In this book, you will read the last time that my father beat me. Even though our parents did beat us, we still always knew that they loved us.

When my sister and I grew up and got jobs, at one time, we worked for the same company. As you know in the winter, it gets dark early, and we worked until 5:30 p.m., It was dark when my father left his job. He would come to our job to pick up my sister and I to take us home so that we would not have to stand and wait for a bus to get home. This was in the early 1950s, and it was safe for us to take the bus. But he didn't want his girls taking a bus when he could pick us up. This is how much he loved us.

My mother taught my sister and I how to love fine clothes, and that is why we still, to this day, dress well and get many compliments because of her.

Living two doors from the church was very good. I spoke about Deacon Jimmerson, but we also had a wonderful Deaconess Maurice Ficklin Riley of Mount Calvary Baptist Church who took up so much time with young people to help them grow into fine young girls and young women. She helped shape my life. By the time I was fifteen years old, I was already attending church business meetings and baptisms, and signing my name to their baptism certificate including signing my name on her husband's certificate. In recent years, I have told one of Maurice's daughters what an important role her mother played in my life and how much it meant to me.

I am grateful to have had such wonderful godparents as Hattie and Otis Hopkins for they were the best in many ways.

When I was hired for my very first office job, I had the best supervisor that anyone could ask for. Florence and her husband

Richard taught Elijah and I how to enjoy the finer things in life such as going to New York Broadway shows and going out to eat in New York where very few colored people were going in the early 1950s. She never made me feel beneath her. She would wear her mink coat, and I in my black coat, and I felt great. She gave me a bridal shower at her home; and when Elijah and I had our first child, she and her husband brought us a washing machine.

Elijah came to New Jersey from Florida when he was ten years old. His parents had ten children, but they always took care of all of them the best that they could. Elijah worked in a grocery store at a very young age. He enjoyed working in a store and worked there until he enlisted into the navy. While working in the store, he was able to help his parents provide extra food for his sisters and brothers since he could bring home bread, cold cuts, and milk, charging it to his little paycheck that he was earning from working in the store. Elijah learned a lot from his boss while working in the store as he taught him how to work hard and how he could achieve a good life. He also found an older woman that he could talk to whenever he needed some advice other than his parents, which we all did from time to time.

The one thing that I liked about Elijah's mother was that she taught all of her children how to wash clothes and other things around the house, not just her daughters but her sons as well.

When Elijah started to date me, his father and one brother did not like me. The reason was that my skin was too dark for them. Elijah's father had dark skin, and he married a woman with very light skin; this is what he wanted for Elijah. Being the person that Elijah was, he knew what he wanted, and he refused to listen to them. I thank him for that as no young girl/woman has ever been loved as I have. Most people think that only white people are like that, but colored/black people, as we are called today, are the same.

Since Elijah and I dated for five years before we got married, his father and the entire family got to know me as the person that I was, and is today, and not by the color of my skin. We all ended up as the best of friends and family.

I wanted to acknowledge the people that played an important role in our lives.

Introduction

My name is Margaret, and I was inspired to write this book when my husband Elijah and I were looking though a large tote and we found our old love letters. These letters dated back sixty-five years, and Elijah was in the navy for four years.

After reading through a few letters, I found one particular letter that was written to me in December 1950. The memories flooded back to me as if I were still that young love-struck girl. I couldn't wait to share this memento with some of my closest friends. I first shared it with Pastor Clark Alexander and his wife Lucina of Graceway Community Church. We had all just finished our Bible study at their home, and the timing was perfect to share such a gem.

I then shared my cherished love letter with a group of ladies from our church, and they thoroughly enjoyed my reading it to them. A few of our friends suggested that I write a book so more people could enjoy the experience of a couple's love that still burns bright after sixty-five years.

Elijah and I believe that sharing our story may reach other couples while encouraging those who may just be starting their journey.

Introduction

Sixty-Five Years of Love

This love story began February 26, 1950 on a Sunday afternoon when Elijah visited me at my home.

We had been talking to each other before this day since we attended the same school in South Side High Newark, New Jersey.

We lived around the corner from each other. I could stand in my kitchen and say good night or talk to Elijah after he had taken me home from a date. He would stand on his back porch and me in my kitchen and wave goodnight.

Some weeks before that Sunday afternoon, my sister Catherine and I attended a graduation party given by Elijah's sister Iona. We were invited as Iona and Catherine graduated from the same class. Elijah was there to look after Iona's guests as her godmother requested. She wanted one of Iona's brothers to be there to assist her guests and to make sure that everything would be all right.

Elijah wanted to get to know me better, so he asked if he could walk us home after the party; and I said yes, of course.

As my birthday was approaching and I was not allowed to date until I turned sixteen, I was given a sweet-sixteen party. Elijah attended my party, and that was the beginning of our sixty-five-year love story.

Early Dates

E lijah and I dated on Sunday afternoons only as we both were going to high school and Elijah had a part-time job.

We went on dates with other couples for only a short time as the other couples wanted to find a house where we all could have sex. Elijah and Margaret were not into having sex as she had just turned sixteen and much too young. By not continuing our dating with other couples, we were not under any peer pressure to do what they were doing.

Before breaking off going on dates with other couples as a group, we all went to New York City. After missing the early bus back to Newark, New Jersey, we arrived back home very late around midnight.

Elijah wanted to walk me up to my third-floor apartment. I said that it was not necessary since I was inside the building, and it was safe in the 1950s. This was a total mistake as my father was very upset when I walked thru the door. My father beat me for coming home late, which was wrong of him since we had not done anything wrong.

The next day, Elijah called to speak to me and spoke instead to my mother who told him that my father had beaten me for coming home late. Elijah told her that we had not done anything wrong, only missed the early bus. Elijah was so upset when he heard what had happened. He said that he would never date me again as my father was crazy.

As luck would have it, Elijah and my father would end up on the same bus to go downtown Newark and came face to face with each other. Elijah told him that we had not done anything wrong, only missed the bus to get home on time. My father said "okay" after hearing the same thing that I had told him.

Elijah spoke to an older woman friend of his that worked in a restaurant. He would go to talk to her as she was married with children and a wise woman that helped to guide him into becoming a nice young man. Elijah told her what had happened on his last date with me. She advised him to go back, continue to date me, and prove to my father that we had not done anything wrong. Remember, I am still sixteen. Many years later, we found out why my father was so upset about me coming home late. My Aunt Bee's boyfriend Jeff was telling him that we had run off to get married, and my father believed him.

There was one more incident that almost broke up our relationship with each other. One Sunday afternoon, he decided that maybe we would like some ice cream. He went to the store to buy some; only he came back two hours later. It turned out that he ran into his brother Sherman, who had dates with two girls at the same time, and needed Elijah to cover for him until he could get rid of one of them. I told him to take his ice cream, go home, and not to come back to see me again. This time, it was my mother that saved him and asked me to give him another chance, which I did; and I am very, very happy that I did.

Our dates consisted with us going to Mount Calvary Baptist Church in Newark, New Jersey; Coney Island, New York; movies; and lots of walks downtown Newark. It was mostly just the two of us as we did not go out on dates with other couples anymore.

Elijah and Margaret as Teenagers
(November 1950)

Margaret's Vacation

On December 1950, my father asked me if I would like to go on a trip to Albany, Georgia, so that I could visit his parents and other relatives. I was excited about going on a trip on a train and by myself. I asked him if he would buy me some new clothes, and he said yes. Also, this trip is more expensive than he had planned, but it was still a go. Being sixteen and traveling was great because it showed me that my father had trust and faith in me.

The last time that I had seen his parents was when his family and my mother's family lived in Blakely, Georgia. At that time, I was seven years old. Since that time, my father's family had moved to Albany, Georgia.

Elijah and I had been dating for ten months when I went on this trip, and he missed me very much.

Because I was missed so much by Elijah, he wrote me a letter while I was in Georgia. This letter was packed away until now, sixty-five years later.

First Romantic Letter to Margaret

259 Broome Street
Newark, New Jersey
December 20, 1950

Dearest Darling,

Darling, I really do believe the Lord created you for me to love. He picked you out from all the rest of the girls because he knew I'd love you best. I once had the heart both brave and true, but now it's gone from me to you. Take care of it, darling as I have done, for you have two and I have none.

If I go to heaven before you do, I'll make room for you on a golden chair; and all the angels will know and see exactly what we mean to each other.

If you are not there by judgment day, I'll know you've gone the other way; and just to show my love for you so true, I'll even go to hell just to be with you.

I am sorry I didn't write you a day sooner, but I had homework to do. I hope you are having a nicer time then I am having.

Written with love
Signed from my heart,
(Mr. Elijah Porter)

P.S. Please come back to me; it's cold up here.

Picture of Margaret

Elijah's Navy Story

From February 1950 until 1951, Elijah and I were having a great time dating.

One afternoon, Elijah stopped by my mother's place of business, which was a beauty parlor. During his conversation with her, he began telling her that he had enlisted into the navy but had not yet told me. He was surprised as I was sitting the back of the shop and had heard every word that he had said. We laughed about it, and there were no hard feelings that he was telling my mother before telling me. I was seventeen years old, and I felt that this was his decision.

Elijah was in the navy from June 1951 until June 1955, when he was discharged. He came home on leave whenever he could. He got extra leave time for New Years as I wanted him to come home for New Years instead of Christmas.

Norfolk, Virginia, area was very prejudiced during the 50s. Whenever the crew from the ship was going to Virginia Beach, Elijah, who was colored—as that was what we were called at that time—was not allowed to go onto the beach. Colored people were not called black until the mid-60s. Because of this, Elijah never had a problem asking for New Years leave instead of Christmas. This was another way of Elijah showing his love for me as I wanted him home for New Year's Eve—one of the most important evenings to go on a date with the person that you love.

When Elijah first joined the navy, I was still attending high school. I graduated from South Side High, Newark, New Jersey, then went on to attend a one-year course at Newark Prep School, Newark, New Jersey, to further my education in business.

June 1952, Elijah asked my father if he could ask me to marry him. Now I was eighteen years old. My father said that it would be all right with him if this was what I wanted. Elijah did purpose to me, and we became engaged for three years until he was discharged from the navy.

Elijah and I did not want to get married while he was in the navy as again, for colored wives to travel with a military husband would have been extremely hard for an eighteen- or nineteen-year-old woman away from home and her family. Elijah was still showing his love for me and did not want me to be mistreated, and he could not be there, to protect me as the ship was constantly on the move, never stayed in one place for too long.

As you read further into the book, you will find out a lot more about Elijah's navy life and how we led our lives during the four years, leading up to his discharge and our marriage.

Letters and Pictures (1951)

April 10, 1951

Dear Margaret,

I am sorry it had to be so soon. I just couldn't help from enlisting into the Navy. I wanted to go ever since I came to South Side High School. Maybe you can't understand, but going into the Navy will make it possible for me to experience a little bit of life before I get married. If I go and come back safe and sound, I wouldn't mind getting married, but now I can't because I haven't anything to offer you.

Maybe when I come back, I'll have enough money to give you the big wedding that you want. Margaret, please don't feel sad or unhappy; just stay as you are, nice and cheerful. When you went south for Christmas in December 1950, I told you that I loved you and always will. Well, that is true; and no water, land, nor bullet can separate what I can't explain, but I really love you until the day I die. You many think that I am crazy. Well, if you fell in love for the first time, you would seem crazy too.

I'll see you tomorrow if I can make it.

Crazy love,
Porter

June 27, 1951

Dear Margaret,

Since you have gotten my card, a lot of things have been happening to me. I have a Navy haircut, Navy food, and Navy shots. The commanding officer said that the Navy would make a man out of me. If they do, that'll be the best thing since the telephone.

Margaret, I am not homesick, and I don't miss anybody. The only person I miss is you. I am with a lot of nice fellows and we get along like peas in a can. Margaret, Navy life is great, and I think I can change now that I am away and can think clearly and get the real understanding of life. It's a long way from home, but I am not even thinking about home. It seems that I miss you more than the hair on my head. I have never been away from you, and now that I am away, I hope you'll understand why I spent all my time with you. I am just writing you this letter to be doing something. I had three shots in my arm and will be getting some more. My arm is sore and tired, but I can stand the pain.

The reason this letter has no outside address is because I am always on the go. I can tell you where I am but you can't write me because that's just a recruiting station. I am located on the Great Lakes. Now I must report to the mess hall for chow (Navy food).

I love you more then you'll ever know. I will write when I get my address. Be sweet and be cool, my love.

Sincerely yours,
Recruiter Elijah Porter

Up at 5 o'clock run from 5 o'clock to 9:30 at night. I mean, you are on the go all the time.

I love you.
I love you.

I love you.
I love you.
I love you.
I love you.

Elijah carried this picture of Margaret for four years while he was in the navy.

June 29, 1951

My Dearest Darling,

The last time I wrote you, I told you I missed you a lot. Now every time I go to bed, I look at your picture until go to sleep. All the fellows like the picture of you on the church steps, but all of them you take are lovely. Margaret, you really don't love a person until you are separated from them.

My new address on the cover will tell you where I am. Margaret, there is no need for me to lie to you or myself, but I do love you. I have found out a little about life. Life in the Navy is what you make of it. I will be training for eleven weeks and going to school at night, so don't feel bad toward me for not writing because I know you'll understand.

Tell Catherine I am still looking for her a Navy boyfriend. Give my regards to your family and Mrs. Hattie.

Well, Margaret, that's about all for now I have so much to say, but I don't have the time to say it. So long, and remember I love you with all my heart, and I have made up my mind of what to do when I get out of the Navy in four years (wedding bells).

Sincerely yours,
Lovingly yours,
E. Porter

June 30, 1951

Dear Margaret,

My heart is feeling like a rock while I am writing you. I have just finished washing five pair of pants, six shirts, two pairs of shorts, and two pairs of leggings. After that, I just had to sit down and write to you.

We were going to drill all day, but it was called off because our commander went to train another recruit.

Margaret, I have to go to church every Sunday. I know you like that. Join the Navy and you can go to church every Sunday.

I was talking with a fellow yesterday, and he told me of what had happened to him the last night he was home. He said his girl cried when he left home and wanted to come with him. I didn't tell him how you acted when I left. Margaret, how did you really feel when I left you that night? What I felt, I'll tell you. I felt like you were leaving me for good. My mouth became dry, and I almost let a tear out of my eye. Don't tell anyone, but some nights, I cry myself to sleep. I know that a man is not supposed to cry, but when you feel like I do, you just can't help from crying. I have held it as long as I can, and now it must show itself on the outside. I just think of all the good times that we have had together.

Margaret, my heart is only a piece of flesh, and I hope you love it as much as I do for I love you with all of it. Margaret, I must go off to deliver mail, but I will write you some more next week.

Yours forever,
Elijah Porter

Post cards when Elijah was in the navy during boot camp.

July 2, 1951

Dear Margaret,

Before, when I wrote to you, I couldn't tell you all the things that was happening here. Now I can tell you a little of the things that is going on. There are about one thousand boys here, and I am the only colored boy. The fellows are nice, and I don't feel unwanted because they all treat me very nice. None of them are from Newark, New Jersey. They come from all over the United States, Europe, Alaska, Canada, and all over.

Margaret, if anybody asks you what I am, tell them I am a Recruit Petty Officer. I'll explain that some other time.

I sent Melba a card but I don't think it was the right address, so if you would send me her address along with some others, I would appreciate it.

Melba Robinson, Rev. J. W. Mapson, Governor Ware, Robert Stevens, Mrs. Ella Grant, Annette Bonner. It's not that I did not know the addresses; it's that I forgot them.

Today, I got my first gun. I named it Margaret, after you. Every time I shoot it, I say, "Nice girl, Margaret."

One day after school, when I finish training, I am going to write you a very long letter and tell you how I feel when I write to you and when you write to me. I get the letters first because I am also the mailman for all the men in my company. Margaret, tell Pete hello and to stay out of the Army and join the Navy.

Well, this about all the room on this paper I have now. If I write any more, I'll be paying for two letters. I love you, baby. Please wait for me.

Sincerely,
Porter E.

Elijah named his gun "Margaret."

July 2, 1951

Dearest Elijah,

While sitting down in deep meditation, I decided that I would answer your letters. When your most adorable letters reached me, they found me in the best of health. I hope when these few lines reach you, you will be the same.

I hope you aren't showing that picture with me in the kitchen holding a bowl of eggs.

I am glad that you finally have your address because I wanted to write to you so badly. Elijah, promise me that whenever you are home, please come and see me because I miss you so much that I could die without you.

Was happy to hear that you like the Navy and that the fellows are nice. The family also sends their love to you. Elijah, remember what I told you; don't be a big showoff, act human and like a mature man.

Are you sure about what you said about (wedding bells)? Remember to be sure before you make a decision that you will want to change.

Elijah, please don't think that I can't keep anything to myself, but I took the gift around to let your family see it, and the letter was in the large envelope and your sister Viola read it to the family. I hope you don't mind. After all, they have to find out sooner or later. I love the gift so much that I have been showing it to everybody.

Always remember that I love you with all my heart. I must close now for it is late.

All of your friends are asking about you and miss you. All that I can do is wait for the mailman.

Affectionately yours,
Margaret Williams, Your Sweetheart
Love & Kisses

July 5, 1951

Hi Margaret,

Today, I got a taste of real Navy life. Every one of the boys in my company got shots in their arms for protection against malaria. While I am writing this letter, I can see them all lying in bed, and it's not even time to go to bed. They are all screaming in pain. Well, you know me. I'm laughing and having fun. You see, I had the same shot before, and it didn't even bother me. They wonder why I'm not bothered with it. If you don't hear from me in a week, you will know why (smile).

Margaret, I started to call you on the 4th of July, but I remembered that you were going to Atlantic City. I was feeling pretty low, so I thought I'd call you. Margaret, if you came up here, everyone would know who you were. I've shown them your picture and talked about you so much they could not miss you.

Being away from you really gets me down. If you love me like I love you, I think you'll understand. I can't explain it too much, but I'll try. Everything I did with you, everywhere we went together keeps coming back like a dream. I remember the last Sunday with you like I remember my name. I am listening to the recording of "I Want to Be With You Always." You remember the one I was talking about before I left. That record makes me think of you like you were here beside me now.

Your picture seems like you are looking out at me from a mirror. When I have time, I look at them. Every time I look at your picture, you seem to be getting prettier and prettier. This is not B.S. but you can believe me if you want, or you can even disbelieve me. You have the right. I am only who you think I am and nothing more.

Margaret, my arm is getting me now so I must sound off. I'll be seeing you.

Love you always,
E. Porter

July 5, 1951

Dearest Darling,

I received that most precious card that you sent to me. I hope that isn't what you will be saying at the end of your four years.

Elijah, you almost didn't have me anymore because Irving tried to drown Iona and me. I went up and down in the water three times. The last time that I went down, I caught somebody's leg and pulled myself up to keep from drowning.

If I hadn't done this, I would have drowned on the 4th of July, and you would not have seen me ever again. Please don't worry; I am fine now.

Love you,
Margaret
1

---

[1] When Elijah read the letter, he was in Cuba. He ran quite a way to find a telephone to make sure that I was all right.

July 6, 1951

Dear Elijah,

I am writing this letter to let you know that I just received your beautiful pillowcase. Pretty soon, I can start a young five-and-dime store. (smile)

Because you put the wrong address on the package, I almost didn't receive it. The man at the grocery store had it and was about to send it back as he didn't know my name.

I like it and appreciate it very much, but can't you ever do anything but spend your money on me all the time?

Your brother Sherman is leaving for the Air Force tomorrow, July 7, 1951. He said that he would write to you as soon he gets stationed.

Your dear sweet darling Margaret (that's me) has a job at last. I found it today, making electric cords. I like it very much. Iona has a job at the pocketbook factory with your cousin.

Love and kisses,
Be good like I told you.
Margaret
XXXXXXXXXXXXXXXXXXXXXX

July 6, 1951

Hi Margaret,

I have your letter beside me while I am writing to you. That is what I was waiting for. It kind of made me feel happy all over. I was more than glad to receive a letter from you. Why do you still write at night? Is it because you dream more or think more?

Margaret, I forgot to tell you that my picture was June 25th issue of the New York Daily News.

I am not angry with you for showing my family the letter or the handkerchief. It is better that you tell them because I don't have the heart to tell them about us. Anyway, it would take too long if I started.

Margaret, every day, I become sure and surer that you are the only girl for me. I really meant what I said about Wedding Bells. If I told you how much I loved you, you would be listing for hours. When I'm lonely, I need you only because you are like a rose in the middle of June. Your picture is like a Margaret Charm. It seems to put me in a deep gaze every time I look at it (every day). It makes me remember you as the girl I left behind

Iona wrote me and told me that you, Irving & Catherine, and her were going to Atlantic City. In my previous letter, you will find out about my July 4th. I hope you had a lovely time. Next time you write me, tell me about it.

Margaret, don't think I am a showoff, but the boys like the picture of you with the bowl of letter, I mean eggs, best.

When I get home, you are my second stop. Can I kiss you in front of your mother? (smile) There is a letter in the mail for you. I'll write you every week even if I have to write in the dark.

Well, my love, I have no more room, so I'll cast up the anchor and set out on the seven seas.

Elijah Porter
XXXX=4X I love you
XXXXX+X=I love you
XXXXXXXXXXXXXX=Love

July 1951

My Dearest Darling,

Today while I read your letter, I couldn't help for remembering you as a little girl. I mean like you were January 1, 1951. If you remember that this little sentence that follows is true, you'll be OK.

I am persuaded that neither death nor life nor angels nor principalities nor powers nor things present nor things to come nor height nor depth nor any other creature shall be able to separate us from the love of each other. Only God knows how much we mean to each other.

Margaret, if you believe in something and pray for something and have someone else believing and praying for the same thing, it will come true. It is written, so shall it be.

Margaret, you never do fully realize that you love someone until one of them goes away. If you feel like I do, you can know how I felt when you went south for Christmas. When you went that week, I felt as you do now but only worse. I know how I feel, but you never did tell me how you felt. That's one trouble with you; you never tell me anything until we are apart. You always keep me hanging by my neck. Then when you got me where you want me, then you tell me. Margaret, that's not fair to my heart. My heart is only a very important thing in my body. If it is broken, so is our love.

Margaret, if I kissed you in front of your mother, would it be all right if I didn't stop kissing you (smile)? Tell me something, why do you still call me Elijah? The fellows up here don't even know my first name. They only know Porter. Being me, the mailman, they can't find out my first name; but if you want to call Elijah, it's okay. I just wanted to know why you always called me by my first name. I know it's a lovely day, I mean name; but when you say (dearest), well, that's different. You can call me Rag Mop; it's all right with me.

I always will if you want me to. I will be home between September 15th and the 25th.

Love you,
Elijah Porter
2

---

[2] Elijah never liked his first name, and everyone called him Porter. Even today, his name is Porter.

August 22, 1951

Hi Margaret,

I received your letter and was very glad to get the answer I was longing for. I have been waiting to hear from you. I really got myself a lovely girl when I got you to tell me why. I didn't know you long before February 26, 1950.

You are always telling me to be a man and act like myself, and I had to get my head knocked off before I came to my senses. They say, "Live, learn, teach, and observe all obstacles in your perceptions." Well, I like to be taught when you are doing the teaching.

I hope what I write to you doesn't worry your pretty head too much. Worrying makes you worry more. So don't worry. I will be alright.

Margaret, about three weeks from now, you will receive a letter from me telling you not to write me anymore. Well, when you do, don't get excited. That will just let you know that I'll be home soon. The reason you will not be able to reach me so that if I do write you one of these letters, don't get yourself up into a turmoil.

Love you,
Elijah Porter

August 29, 1951

Hi Margaret,

I received your most adorable letter just a few seconds ago. I was overjoyed hearing from you. I have been very busy since the last time I wrote to you. They are filming a movie up here about the waves and our CO. 575 is to take part in it. Maybe you can get a chance to see it when it is released. If you do, look out for CO 575, and maybe you'll be lucky enough to see me. There are sailors in this picture that maybe you won't see me, but don't worry. I'll be there some place. This will make the third picture that's been made since I have been here, but the first one we are taking part in.

The reason you can't see the ring is because I don't have it. When I leave here, I may lose it, or it may get borrowed and never returned on the train. I will let you see it when I come home, I want to be sure that your mother and father say OK before I buy it. If you like, you can come with me to buy it. If you like, then you could pick out the one you like best; or if you rather that I use my own judgment, that's OK too.

If I think that you are a perfect angel, then to me, you are. I don't know what other people think, but to me, you are a perfect angel. I'll have to find out for myself if you aren't.

When I do come home, I'll be wearing my dress uniform, blue with two stripes on my sleeves, white for deck crew and three on my cuffs for national purposes. The white uniform is only a summer one. When I leave here, it will be kind of cold. It is already getting a little humid. The uniforms that I have are the right size too; they fit me like a glove. I think that they are better looking than any other Armed Forces uniforms, don't you? What I do hope when I come home is that everybody doesn't make a fuss over me. When some service men go away and come back for a visit, everybody makes you feel like a hero, and you haven't been outside of the States. I just want to see you.

Margaret, while I am there, then maybe I'll spend some time with my family. I have so much to talk to you about that I want a lot time with you. I must go now. The chow runner has just left, and we must fall out on the grinder for chow.

So be sweet like you always have and keep looking happy. I'll be seeing you soon.

Yours Eternal,
Elijah Porter

P. S. My birthday is Sunday, September 2. Save my present until I get home. I'll collect it in kisses.

September 2, 1951

Dearest Elijah,

While sitting down, thinking of such a sweet person, I decided to write to him. I hope when this letter reaches you, you will be in the best of health.

I wish you the most Happiest Birthday that you have ever had.

The families are well, and everybody is dying to see you. Sherman was home today on your birthday; he looks good. I can't say that much for you as I haven't seen you yet (smile).

Do you think that you will be home on September 21, 1951 for the crowing of Miss Mount Calvary to be held then because it had been postponed? Hope you will also be able to see me in my gown.

Did you know that we are getting married this month? This is what is being told by a girl who lives downstairs in the same building that I live in. She has put out information that you and I are getting married as soon as you get home. People know more about your business than you know yourselves.

[3]Iona, Catherine, and I went to the Loews Theater today; and it reminded me of when we would go there together.

I will close now.

Love to My Darling Sweetheart from Your Darling,
Margaret

---

[3] This event was hosted by Mount Calvary Baptist Church Choir, which Margaret was a member. Margaret ended up winning the title of Miss Mount Calvary in 1951.

September 5, 1951

Dearest Darling,

Your letter found me in the happiest time that I could be in. Well, about me coming home, I can't set a special date. I really don't know for sure when I'll be home, but you will know soon.

If a big windbag grabs you and holds you with all its might, then you'll know that windbag will be me. I hope I'll be home for the crowning of Miss Mount Calvary. I would like to see your gown, but for my part, you'd look good in a flower curtain (smile).

Well, I had a lovely birthday. I spent it on the grinder and in the wash (deep sink) all day. Then after that, I played a couple of games of basketball.

You said that Sherman was home; do you know when he'll be home again? Maybe next time when he does come home, I will be there too. I hope you didn't let that bus driver's uniform get you up in the air. If it did, well, good. The Air Force is OK; it's just that the Navy and the Air Force don't speak the same language. We are a nice group, but mostly, all Navy fellows talk about some other branches of services now and then

Margaret darling, you are the only girl that sails my ship. If I couldn't believe in you and could not put all my hope in you, you make me and you can tear me down easier than you made me. So believe me when I say I love you. I lay my life in your hands; do what you like, but do what's best. I love you now and always until the end of time.

I love you.

Yours,
Elijah Porter
4

---

[4] Elijah and his brother Sherman went into the military around the same time. This was why Elijah was saying that the navy was better than the air force.

October 11, 1951

Dearest Darling,

While sitting down thinking of no one but you, I decided that I would write you a letter. I am fine and hope that when this letter reaches you, you will be in the best of health.

The family is well, that is, yours and mine. How do you like it where you are now? I am still working hard. I know you told me not to, but working hard is the only way that I can get what I need and want for January. Please understand that is the only reason that I am doing it because you know how much it means to me.

I wonder what you did to me before you left to join the Navy. Twice, I had dreams that I was crying; and each time, you were there. The first time I dreamed that I was crying, but I didn't know what I was crying about, you came to me, held me in your arms, and told me not to cry anymore. The second time I was crying was because I thought a group of people jumped on you and beat you up, and I was crying and said, "You all didn't have to jump on him. One at a time would have been enough if you have to fight him." What do you make of my dreaming these dreams about you and crying each time as they seemed so real as I were dreaming them? Elijah, you are the very last thing that I think about falling to sleep each night. I love you so much until sometimes I think how I can be away from you.

Do you think for sure that you will be home next weekend? Because Buddy and his club is having a party, and I would enjoy it ten times better if you were there with me than if I just went with the crowd. Last Saturday night, Iona and I went to dance to see Cootie Williams, and I didn't enjoy it at all because you weren't there. You may think that I am lying, but I am not. All the while that I was there, I was wishing that you were there too.

Our club sends their love to you, and everyone asked about you. Don't think hard of me writing on this paper because I am in my study period at school writing this letter. The next one will be on pretty paper just for you.

I love closing with love,
Margaret

November 19, 1951

Hi Margaret,

Wow, what a happy fellow I am today. We just came back today from Puerto Rico. I was so happy that I didn't know what to do because I knew I would get some mail from you, and I did. I got two sweet letters from you and my family. They were what I needed to cheer me up.

How long are we going to stay here in North Carolina, I wouldn't know. We have to pick up a shipload of supplies and then back to the sea. This time, we will be going to the Mediterranean. France and Italy are our main stops. We will be over there for about six or seven months the most. Then we will return to America again. I am sorry that I won't be able to make it home for Thanksgiving. If I could, I would only to get a 72 hour pass from here. It would take that long to get to New Jersey, and I would be two days late coming back to my ship. So please understand why I can't come home this time. I know I want to be home for Christmas or your graduation, but write and tell me about both; and when you get time this Thursday, give a little thanks to God for you being such a nice little girl. When Christmas comes and you start eating that chicken, or turkey, remember that I will be eating the same thing and thinking of you just as you are of me. I sure will be too.

For as long as we have been going together, we haven't spent a Christmas together yet, and this one looks hopeless as a cow jumping over the moon. Margaret, when these holiday days come, have a nice of a time that you can. I want you to even if I am not there, but have yourself a great time because these holidays are like a birthday; they come once a year. So when they do come, they are to be enjoyed and not to be sorrowful. You should try not to think of me so much because, Margaret, I know it's hard for you not to, but try and enjoy yourself like a nice girl.

Margaret, I may not able to send you any presents for the holiday or your graduation. As I said before, we came to pick up supplies. If we don't leave until after our next payday, I'll buy you something and have it shipped to you. That's if we are in the States when payday comes,

I hope that we are, because I really want to give you something nice for your birthday and your graduation.

I know the first thing that you will say is, "Elijah, you don't have to buy me anything." You always tell me that when I say that I'm buying you something.

Love you, my darling Margaret Williams,
Elijah Porter

November 30, 1951

Dearest Elijah,

We are having our Senior Show, Friday, December 7th.

Iona, Catherine and I are going together. We all are also going to a dance tonight which is November 30th.

Graduation will still be dull no matter what you say or tell me to do. The only way that it can be a happy and successful one is that you are here to enjoy it with me.

I won't even have anyone to take me the prom, and if I don't find someone soon, I am afraid that I am not going.

Are you still in North Carolina? If so, do you know how long that you are going to be there, because I am going to send you your Christmas card next week; and I want you to get it before. Otherwise, you might not get it until after Christmas

Goodbye for now.

Your love,
Margaret

December 4, 1951

Hi Margaret,

Your second letter had a lot of things, like dates that are important to you. Some of them that you should remember all of your life, and I'm not there to help you and myself remember them.

Much as I would like to, I am afraid that I won't be there for quite a while. I hope you enjoyed yourself at the dance Friday night. I haven't danced in so long that I think I forgotten how. I was never good at it, and now I'm even worse.

Maybe I can help your graduation and Christmas to be a little enjoyable even if I'm not there. We should be back to Norfolk before Christmas Day. But I still won't be able to come home. Navy regulations, we get 30 days leave every year, and I have already used up 14 of them.

Send my Christmas card anytime. It's OK if I get it late. I want to send yours early and will try to go ashore to buy you something.

I enjoy any kind of letter as long as it is from you. Now I must close because I am getting tired. Bye for now and be sweet like a good girl. Santa Claus will be good to you this Christmas.

I love you, Margaret.

Elijah Porter

December 27, 1951

Dearest Darling,

I received your lovely Christmas card on Christmas Day. It was very nice, and I like it very much. Only I am sorry that I couldn't make the message on it come true. I started to answer you when it came, but after dinner, I couldn't write very good. I think that I ate a little too much turkey at one time. I slept until 1200, then I got up and ate again. We had a lot of assorted foods and nuts.

Christmas day with me this year was just like last year. Only this time, it is vice versa. Only you are the one that is staying, and I am the one that is away now as I did then. But this time, I felt worse than I did. Then there were a lot of people aboard, but I felt like I was alone. I think I was in more ways than one. I sure was lonely too. I didn't tell you why I was so low did I? Well, we had some cigars we bought down in Bermuda. I tried one, and I don't think I will again. I tried it just to be doing something for enjoyment, but I didn't know a cigar could taste so bad.

This is about all for now. I got to secure some lines before taps. But when I get some more time to write, I will try to catch up on some of my writing.

It's been quite a while since I wrote to you a very long letter. Well, Margaret, I hope to be hearing from you, my darling. I will always feel the same way about you.

Darling,
Elijah Porter

December 28, 1951

Dearest Darling,

I received your letter and was very glad to hear from you. I am fine and hope when you receive this letter and you open it, you will be the same.

Iona, Drew and I went to the station with Sherman tonight to see him off. I don't like that job. If I go the train station, I want to be going on the train myself, going somewhere. Do you think that we will ever take a train trip together one day?

For graduation, you can send me anything that you want to or nothing at all. It will still be OK. I was very grateful for what you sent to me for Christmas.

About the tattoo, if you feel as though you would like to have one, go ahead and get it. The only thing that matters to me is that you are happy and doing the thing that you want to do, so go ahead and have whatever you want, I don't ever want for you to say if it wasn't for me, you would have done such and such. So please do whatever you want if you think that it would make you happy.

Forever yours,
Margaret
5

---

5 Elijah never did a get tattoo.

Letters and Pictures (1952)

January 8, 1952

Dearest Darling,

I received your letter today and was very glad to hear from you. I hope when this letter reaches you, it will find you and your family in the very best of health.

I couldn't answer it before we sailed. So now I know you will get this letter a little late. But just the same, I still thought I would write you to let you know I am still thinking of you and loving you just as much as ever.

Maybe when we are together once more, never to part, maybe then, we can take a train trip together or some long vacation. When that happens, then you won't have to be waiting on the platform, but I don't think I would like you to see me off again. The last time was enough. I still remember that day. I think my heart took that train ride instead of me. It's just that I wanted to stay with you a little longer than I did, but my time was limited. When I do come home again, I hope time doesn't pass as fast as it did.

When you graduate, we will be out to sea some place. I hope you have a very happy one and all the luck and fun that come with it.

I was thinking about getting a tattoo when I wrote you that letter the other time. Now, since your last letter, I have changed my mind until I get another bright idea. Don't get me wrong. I still may or may not get one; the chances are I won't. You know I am always getting some smart brainy idea. When a person gets tattoo, it takes a long time for them to heal because the top of the skin is open to the colored ink that they use. Then when they are finished, sometimes they look good; then again, they don't.

Margaret, you told me to take good care of myself so that you will have someone and something to wait for. Well, I am taking good care of myself to the very best that I can, and I hope you are doing the same because I feel the same way as you do. I wouldn't want anything to happen to you. I am a long way from you, and if anything did happen, I wouldn't know what I would do. I lay awake at night and wonder if you are alright, or is there something the matter with you. You are so sweet. In all my dreams, your face appears in them like the sun in the morning. You warm my heart like the sunlight warms the flowers in spring time.

I miss you more and more. Even if I can't be with you, I can still be by myself with the memories of you. They seem old now because I haven't seen you in three months to get any new ones, but just the same, I like them. As long as they are about you, that's all that matters to me. I don't think about anything or anybody but you, and I don't want to if I can't think about you. You are my darling, and I hope you will always remain my darling. As long as you are, I will live in memories as well as in real times.

Margaret, I will close now, and I hope that you believe what I have written. I think you will because if you love me as I do you, you will.

So long, my Darling
Elijah Porter

Elijah
(High School)

Margaret
(High School)

Margaret
Graduation from High School
(1952)

January 22, 1952

Dearest Darling,

I hope when you receive this letter, it will find you very healthy and happy. I am fine and a little lonely now that I am a few hundred miles away from you. I sure wish that I were a few inches instead of a few miles. I hope you were not worrying too much about me. We wrote letters on our way over here, but they never left the ship. I sure do hope you get one of these letters so that you will know where I am. Then, you won't have to worry your little head off about me. I am all right even if you don't hear from me for quite a while. If you thought about me as much I thought about you, then I know that you didn't get much sleep because all the way over here, I was think-ing about you and how much fun we once had. I wonder if we ever will have as much fun together in the future as we have had in the past. I never knew a person could miss any person as I miss you. The days were OK, but the nights, when all the lights were out and only the stars to shine, I did a lot of dreaming and looking at the stars and dreaming. I wished that you could have been there by my side so that you could have felt the same as I did, and still had, yesterday.

I took out all of your pictures and looked at them until I went to sleep. Your old letters, then, I reread them over for the hundredth time, sounded better than they did the first time that I read them. When I read them, I thought you were reading to me and not myself rereading what you said a long time ago. It may not have been so long but how slow time travels.

A couple days ago, we were in Spain. That's a very lovely coun-try. We heard some Spanish music while we were there, and the sound was nothing like the old USA. It was lovely, but I still go for the music I can understand. They sang American songs in Spanish so good that if a person was a bad person after listening to that music, I think they would turn into a better person altogether. We didn't have much time to spend there because we were still moving. One day was all we could spend there; it was spent well too. We, I mean myself, just went sightseeing about the city. Right now, I couldn't tell you because I have forgotten. It was a Spanish name anyway for 80 cents. I had myself a nice time looking the place over. You know something; you could never tell that a war was ever over here. The way the people treat you make you feel like you were at a friendly place. I must confess that Spanish music really gets your insides to feel good.

Margaret, I may see a thousand things and hear all the sweetest music there is, but I would rather see and hear your voice than anything. There is this side of heaven because I love you, and even though we may be far apart, I still do and I will always. You are the only person in my life for me, and I know that you will always remain in my heart until I can let you out to hold you in my arms once more for keeps and not for a little while but always.

I guess right about here I will close. Margaret, I don't know how long it takes mail to get to you, but don't worry too much about me. I am OK and will be OK. Be sweet, my baby.

Yours,
Elijah Porter

January 23, 1952

Dearest Elijah,

While sitting down with nothing else to do, I decided that I would write you even if I can't receive any mail from you. I am doing pretty good and hope when you receive this letter, you will be the same.

Irving left for the Air Force this morning. Everybody is going into the service. What are we poor girls going to do?

Graduation is Wednesday, January 30th. I wish that you were here with me. We had Senior Day on the 17th of January. I received the money for your pictures, and I got them Saturday when they were ready and they look wonderful, ten times better than the proofs. I couldn't get you a yearbook because it was too late when I got the money.

Here are two of your pictures. If you don't want them, kindly send them back.

Write more next time.

To my darling Elijah,
Margaret

January 24, 1952

Dearest Darling,

I received your lovely letter today and was very glad to hear from you. I haven't heard from you in so long that this letter was what I needed to cheer me up inside, and it sure did all the way.

New Year's was all right, but I would like to have spent it there with you now. As I write this letter, it seems like there wasn't any Christmas or New Years for me. They were just like any other days of the year. I wouldn't have mind to have been at the Masonic hall with you. I know if that man had kept bothering you when I was there, I would have given him the word to leave you alone. Maybe it's a good thing that I do have a controllable temper. If I didn't, I could get myself in a lot of trouble for giving people the word about pestering you when you don't feel like being bothered.

I am glad to hear that your father's deal came out OK. Now when I come home, I will have to find out where Littleton Avenue is. Say where is that anyway? I think I know about where it is, but I am not sure. I haven't been there in so long that my mind is a little bit forgetful when it comes to addresses. I still can remember yours in my sleep and write you name in my sleep.

Margaret, when we get married, we can have a little cozy house of our own, then we can catch up on some of the things that we missed while we were apart. Now when we do get married. Until then, I will be needing you just as much as I will need you until then.

I think I could make you very happy, Margaret, and I know you would make me a lucky and happy fellow in this world. I could never, in my whole life, find another girl that I could love and care for as I do you. I wouldn't want to look for any other because I know I wouldn't find her. I found in you all the things I have been looking for all my life. Margaret, when this is all over and I come home to stay, then we can make all the plans we want like this. We make them and hope for the best. I hope yours and mine come true. I have made some myself, but every time I tell them to you, they turn out wrong. This Navy life sure can make things screwy when I make them. Now I make sure this dog gone. Navy isn't in them. I only want to make sure of things and that they all have you in them too.

I want to marry you, Margaret; I want to get engaged to you. And this time, no family is going to stop me. I know what I want, and nobody else has anything to say. I just know I want you now and for always. That's all that matters. Bye now and be a sweet little girl. Love you.

Elijah Porter

February 6, 1952

Dearest Darling,

Taken time off from my other duties today. I thought I would write you just to let know that I am still in one piece and fine, and I hope you are the same.

In a few days from now, it will be February 8th, your birthday. I know you will get this letter way after it, but I am still going to wish you a very happy one and many more to come. Then after, that will be February 26th. It seems like everything happens in February. What happens to you and I are all nice and very wonderful. This month is full of old times and places. What I would like to have is not sit and remember but to sit and look at you. That would be better than all the memories to me. I hope you didn't think I had forgotten you. How could I? It's just that we move about a lot now and do a lot of work late at night that a person can't hardly find time to write as much. When I do, I start then give up because I can't seem to put my thoughts into words. You know how a person gets when they are doing more dreaming than work. I do more dreaming than I do work. Maybe it's because I miss you more each day. When I feel that way, I just want to be alone. That way, I feel and think better.

Most of the time, I go ashore. I go alone. The people over here don't bother you if you mind your own business. They are just like the people back home, only a different way of living. They talk the same way we do. Sometimes, they even surprise me with the American jive. The one word all of them seem to know is "Be cool." The fellows seem to know that better than the older ones. I think they are more up-to-date than we are in everything except the music. Did you know that Cow Cow Boggy is a top recording here in Pom Pey? Spain was the only country that I have visited so far that was on the ball with top, latest recordings.

I am trying to find you a birthday gift while I am over here. That's the only way I can get rid of this Italian money. You can't give it away. I will be seeing you in my next letter.

So, Margaret, be sweet and take care of yourself.

Bye, my Darling,
Elijah Porter

P.S. I love you now and for always.

February 7, 1952

Dearest Darling,

While sitting down re-reading your letter, I decided that I would write you since I haven't written to you in such a long time. I am fine and hope when you receive this letter, you will be the same.

On graduation, I had a lovely time. I finally made the score that I wanted to make in graduating. After graduation, Melba, Perry and his brother, and I went to New York to Bird Land; we had a lovely time. I had my first Tom Collins, and I didn't like it too well because it tasted like water with lemon juice mixed in it.

I got home at 3:30 in the morning, and I didn't get a hollering at or a beating this time. I would have enjoyed twice as much if you were there to share it with me. Tomorrow, February 8th, is my birthday.

For graduation, I received a watch from my mother, $5.00 from my mother's landlord, a set of sweaters from my cousin Charlie, a pair of shoes and a bag from Ms. Maggie, a gown from Mrs. Hattie, and a dollar and a quarter from a lady on my job.

Elijah, I am sorry but I forgot to ask you if there any racial discrimination in the Navy. Carrol Wilson asked me to write and ask you because he wants to join but heard that there were some. Please answer right back and let me know.

Here is a picture of a party that I went to for graduation. Remember February 26th? We will have been dating for two years. I still love you and always will.

Closing with all my love

Your Darling Sweetheart,
Margaret

February 10, 1952

Dearest Darling,

While lying here wondering and thinking of what you may be doing now that you are out of school. The only way I can find out is to write and ask, so here I am.

I heard all about your graduation from beginning to end, the way Howard, my pal, described. It made me feel as I was there too. He told me all about Senior Day and everything that he could think of. Too bad he doesn't know you. If he did, maybe he could have told me how you looked while all this excitement was going on. But I guess he had enough girls of his own to worry about. Maybe you heard about this guy who kissed all the girls in his homeroom. He was the boy I bet some fellows didn't like. I also had one of South Sides papers. You see, I did keep up with the news about South Side. Too bad they lost the last basketball game that they played.

Augusta Sicily is a pretty nice place to live if you like living in California. They both are about the same. There are some nice small houses there that sit on the side of hills. All along the shore, you can see old ruins that were there from a long time before we came here. Every time I see the beautiful places, they remind me of the day you and I went to the park, the last day I was a civilian. All the time, my mind keep saying all of that will come again. I hope it will, or when I am out on the sea all alone, I want to see some of the things that I used to see with you. The stillness of the night really works on a person's nerves. It wouldn't be so bad, but when you look out into the darkness covering you up like a blanket, all this and other things make me fall deeper and deeper in love with you. I think too much about you all day and night that the days seem to go slower. All the sailors have girls back home that they love, and so all we do is talk about them. I do more talking about you. I bet than anything else it comes natural when I have to talk about a person as nice as you are.

Now I have to close this letter for we are getting ready for chow. I have to mail this letter today in order for it to leave the ship on the next mail run.

I will always love you not for just a day but always.

Love,
Elijah Porter

February 12, 1952

Dearest Darling,

I hope when you receive this letter, it will find you just as I am, maybe better. I am great and having a wonderful time moving around here.

Today, I did something I haven't done since I left Little Creek. We got the captain's OK to go ashore for a few games of sports. We went with some Marines. I mean, they went with us. Well, we marched about five miles into the hard of Tarinto before we got to the place where you are to play ball. There was a whole gang of Italians there playing, but when they saw us coming, they moved off because the American Counsel had made the arrangements for us. They sat on the sideline and watched us play first, which was basketball.

The Navy beat the Marines, 64 to 26. The football game was also won by the Navy, 36 to 12. I played baseball while all the other games was going on. We killed them with 10 to 41. Didn't do so bad myself. If I told you how I did, you would think I am showing off again, so I won't tell you (smile). After the whole thing was over, we had a party right there on the ball field.

This place where we played used to be a Roman Arena. It has a wall around it, about 20 feet high, and you probably have seen pictures of it in your high school books. It is one of those places where they feed people to the lions, not now though. If they did, we wouldn't be there.

Then after we left there, we marched down the streets back to the Fleet Landing where we caught a van back to our ship. We really enjoyed that mostly because all of us were worn out from running so much. We had been to sea so long that we never did have a chance to give our muscles a good work out. You should have seen the Navy Officers' faces when we told them the Navy killed the Marines. I know you thought the Navy was going to get beaten. Well, you can never keep the Navy down no matter how hard you try. We are just a hard-fighting outfit; that's all there is to it.

I enjoyed this too because when we left Little Creek, I had a messed-up left hand from playing ball down there. I wrote you, when I was down there, that it took four hours to write. Well, that's why both my hands were messed up. Now they are as good as ever, and I played this game without anything happening to me. Now don't go worrying your pretty little head off. I am OK. That was a long time ago, and I haven't even a scratch on me, so don't worry. I didn't tell you then because you know how women are.

Well, Margaret, I guess I have done enough talking now, so I think I will do like a good sailor would do and sign off. I will write to you from our next port.

So I'll be seeing you in my dreams.

Your Darling,
Jughead Porter

February 21, 1952

Dearest,

I received your lovely letter and card today, and was more than glad to hear from you. I'm writing while I am lying down, so don't think too hard of the writing if you see some errors.

I was happy to hear that you had a lovely time on graduation, so you finally made it. How does it feel to be out of high school now? I bet you wished you were back there (smile).

How is Melba anyway? I wrote her a couple of times, but she never did answer, so I stopped writing now until she writes to me. Tell her hello the next time that you see her. Thanks.

When I first read your letter, I thought Tom Collins was a name of somebody. When I read it over and it's a drink, well, do tell I've heard everything now, a drink named after Thomas Collins, my old friend Tom (smile).

You see now that you are a year older, your Pop doesn't holler at you so much. How does it feel to be a little older? I bet when you hit twenty-one, you are going to start counting backwards, aren't you? That's OK. I still will know how old you are. I think that I wished you a Happy Birthday and Valentine's Day. I have nothing to send to you but my wishes, but until I can do better, will you accept them? The card was lovely; it said just what I want to say to you. But instead, you said them to me. You seem to catch me always sleeping, but I'm going to catch you off guard one day, then *bang*, you will hear things you never thought I could tell you.

The answer to your question is yes. I don't know why my Pop didn't want me to get engaged when I was home. He is a strange person. My Mom didn't saiyanything. She just said I should listen to my Pop. Maybe this time, he will think different if I give him a good long talk, man to man. I think I am old enough to talk man to man

with him now. Well, I am not going to worry about that now. I have
made up my mind.

Here I am signing off now.

Roger, over and out.

Yours,
Elijah Porter

February 26, 1952

Dearest Darling,

I hope when you receive this letter, it will find you happy and enjoying the very best of health.

I am great and having a lot of laughs, if you can call sailing fun, since we left Catania a few days ago and have been sailing around ever since. I thought I would write you today because this day and date means a whole lot to me as this makes two years that we have been going together. I have enjoyed every minute as well as every day. I hope you have too. You have made me very happy in the past, and I hope you will continue to do so in the future. For without you, I am like a ship without a sail, and the stars can't get along if the sky isn't there to hug them when it's time to sleep. You would never think that you are the person who caused me to act and do things as I do. One person can mean a great deal to someone even if they are apart. I can't see you in the flesh, but I can see you in my dreams. I may not be able to hear your sweet voice, but at night, I can hear your echo coming over the sea, clear as a bell. If I closed my eyes real tight, I can see a very nice little girl smiling. I always seem to see you smiling all the time. That's the way I want you to be, smiling.

I forgot to mention in my last letter that picture of you that was taken at that party. You looked very nice. The rest of them did too, but I wasn't too much concerned about them. I bet half of the fellows in your graduation class have joined up for the Armed Forces.

Those poor, poor women and girls. No wonder there is a man shortage back there; and over here, there seem to be a women shortage or something or other. Whatever it is, they are short of it.

Margaret, I was doing a little book reading. The reason was for my other rate. Well today, I found out that I had made it. Sunday, we took the test. Boy, was I happy now. I think I'll let the book rest for a while before I try to go up for another rate. One year is alright with me. That reading is too much; you can't read very well when the letters keep moving around with the moving of the Old Bell Grove is the cause of that. So far, now we have had some very nice sailing weather. Before, when you walked down the passage, you had to be on the lookout for a runaway horse. He would be headed for the side of the old; stomach would be jumping up and down.

Well, I will close this letter. I will be looking for you in your next letters. Bye, Baby.

E. Porter

April 10, 1952

Dearest Darling,

Sitting here thinking and feeling a little sorry, I thought that I would write you. I received your lovely Easter card just as we were leaving a small island as we are in Athens, Greece. I wanted to write you as soon as I received it but couldn't, as we were taking part in a lot of landings. So I couldn't write a very good *letter* if I tried.

The reason I am so low is because I didn't send you an Easter card. I didn't even send you a gift; you must not think much of me now. I tried to get something for you when we were on that island a while back. They didn't have anything good enough for you. It will be after Easter when you get this letter, but you know I am never on time for anything. I should have thought of this date before now. Now it is too late; time goes so slow that I lose track of days and months. I know you should be angry with me; you should not be forgotten about on Easter. It's my fault, and I am to blame. The card you sent to me was very sweet. I believed every word that it said. It was so sweet that it almost made my eyes water.

Margaret, you should not have spent so much money for a card like that. I would have liked a smaller one just as much as I liked this one. You really shouldn't be spending so much money on me when you need it for yourself. Well, that's just one of the things that make me love you as I do.

I do love you so much that it hurt me at times. I mean deep down inside, not to see on the outside but it is there anyway. That's what makes a fellow want to see his girl more and more. I sure want to see you in more ways than one. Maybe when next Easter comes around, I will be enjoying it with you. That would be very nice to spend a whole day, with a girl as nice as you are.

Well, we should be coming home in a few months. When we do, I'll be looking forward to seeing you, so be a real nice girl. Don't let anything happen to you, and take care of yourself for me so I will have someone to come home to.

When we were over in Athens, we saw a swell show. It was all American; everything there was from the States. It made some of the fellows go haywire, but they simmered down when they played the song, "You Belong to My Heart." That's getting to be a very popular song over here. Athens is the only place we have seen that is more modern; everything is different than all the other countries we have seen.

No wonder they call it the City of Cities. It's a swell place for anybody to see. They have an American USO where you can meet people back from the states. All the food you want is free too. That's why I go. All the food you can eat on; yes, bring on the food (smile). I really don't eat as much as I say I do.

Well, Margaret, this looks like all I can think of now. It's getting late, so now I can't find words to write like I used to. I can't even write a four-page letter anymore. I guess it's just that I miss you so much.

Forever yours,
Elijah Porter

April 15, 1952

Dearest Elijah,

I thought that I would write you and give you my new address; it is as the above on this letter.

I am fine and hope when you receive this letter, you will be the same. I received your letter Saturday and was very glad to hear from you.

How was Easter with you? It was pretty good with me but would have been better if you were here with me. Easter Monday I went to the Terrace Ball Room to a dance as we did last year. I saw Edna McGriff who is so beautiful singing "Heavenly Father."

Everyone sends their love to you.

I am still going to night school. Will write more next time.

Did you receive the Easter card that I sent to you?

Your Darling,
Margaret

April 30, 1952

Dearest Darling,

When you receive this letter, I hope it will find you in the best of health. I'm fine and hope that your family is well also.

We will hit France in a few days; I thought I'd write you before we leave.

This is the first time I am writing to you at your new address. How do you like where you live now? It must be nice to leave Prince Street; you wanted to get away from there so bad. I still can't picture that place where you live at now. I can't seem to remember where Littleton Avenue is; it must be quite away from the old place. Your Pop must be really happy too. He told me if I didn't come back in two months, he would have a house. Well, I haven't been in two weeks, and he has his house. How does it look? Someday, maybe we will have a little cozy house of our own.

Maybe in a few more years, we can do more things that we can't do now. Margaret, I want to be home for the 4th of July. If everything works out, maybe I can for a few days if we are in the States.

I will close this letter now and get some sleep. We will have to get up early in order to get off to an early start.

So long, Baby.

Yours forever,
Elijah Porter

May 27, 1952

Dear Darling,

I was thinking about you so much in the past two weeks that I decided that I had better write you a few lines.

I haven't received any mail from you in three weeks. I am doing pretty good and hope you are doing the same.

I am working seven hours a day at National Union Radio Co. and then four and five hours on Tuesday and Thursday evenings at Sibert & Co. where I used to work, and then I go to school Monday, Wednesday and Friday. Then I work seven to eight hours on Saturday for Sibert & Co. Sunday, I go to church, sometimes back to church in the evening; so you see I have a very busy schedule.

Your sister Iona doesn't give me too much time to feel lonely when she is around for she is forever picking on me hugging and kissing me. She said that she is taking care of me for you. Well, she is doing a fine job of it (smile).

Write soon.

Your Darling,
Margaret

June 1952

Dearest Darling Margaret,

There are many things I have told you while I was home. They were as true as my love is for you. Maybe I was going thru things a little too fast, but I only see you a few days in a year then I try to make up for lost time. It's just that when I'm away from you, I feel as though I am all alone.

Margaret, when I told you I love you and always will, I mean that. I will keep telling you. I wouldn't want any other person to be the mother of my children because you are the one for me for the rest of my life. I just want to make you happy. This time, when I go away, it will be a whole lot worse than before. I sure will miss you like I never did before.

As I'm writing this letter; I wish you were here with me. I feel so lonesome. I didn't get home until late last night. I just went walking thru the streets. It was about 1:30 a.m. when I came home, then I still didn't get any sleep. Baby, please write me as often as you can because I will be waiting for your letters to cheer me up. They are what I need when I am so far away from you. I know you won't have much time to write because of the little spare time you have, I understand why you don't write as often as I do; I'll try to write more.

Margaret, I hope you liked the ring that I gave to you because I wanted to. Not because I thought it was the right thing to do but because I wanted you to have it. It didn't cost too much money. Anyway, it was worth every penny of it for you. That may not have been the way you wanted me to give it to you, but Margaret, that one was the best I could think of at that time. I didn't know how your mother and father would react toward me asking them. Now that it's over, it wasn't so bad. Still, I am a little worried. I shouldn't be, but I am. I don't know why, but I am anyway

Margaret, please, please take care of yourself for me. I would die if something happens to you while I am away. I may not have told you before that I worry more about you than anything else. Well, I do. For you are the only reason I want to come home. I'll just wait until I won't have to see you a few days in a year, but every day. Three more years, then maybe I can.

You asked me if there were any rules? Well, there is only one. Keep loving me as you have, and I will love you until death do us part. Then I will love you more even still.

Last night, when I was at your house, I just kept thinking of Thursday so much that I just had to leave you. It was getting on my mind too much. I am sorry if you thought I was a little angry. I was thinking about kissing you goodnight, and soon I would be kissing you goodbye for a long, long time; so I just had to leave.

Margaret, I will always feel this way about you as I truly love you, and I always will and hope that you feel the same way about me.

Well, so long, Baby, you sweet thing.

Yours,
Elijah Porter
U.S.N.

July 10, 1952

Dearest Darling,

I have just finished reading your most adorable letter. Before I tell you what happened, don't laugh. Well, on my way down here, the bus had a little accident; I wasn't hurt. Then after we got going again, two flat tires held us up for two more hours. By this time, the bus reached Portsmouth about 0800, and we couldn't catch the ferry because it was too small. I fell asleep. When I woke up again, it was 10:00. Now we were on our way to the bus station. When I got to the dock, my ship was gone. So I turned myself into the receiving station here on the base. They first took all my identifications from me, then they put me in jail until today. I just got out today, about two hours ago.

I don't ever want to go back in that place again. They treat you like a murderer. I don't think San Quentin could be any worst. At night, you get locked up until 0500 the next morning. All day, men walk around with 45s and make you feel like a criminal. Well, my ship came back today; and Margaret, I am very, very glad to be back on it. It may not be the best ship in the Navy, but it is home for me. Well, you don't have to wait for me (smile). I won't be home for a long time. I can't leave this ship, but that's OK, I don't want too. This is alright with me as long as I am here. They didn't do anything with me or to me. It was just the idea of being locked up. That was the first time I have ever been locked up or even in jail.

Margaret, do me a favor, will you? Don't tell my family what happened. I am only telling you because I promised I would. If not for that, I would not tell you. Maybe it is better this way. I won't be home for a long time now. By that time, maybe some of my family problems will have quiet down.

I am going on 21 years old now, and if I don't start to break away from them now, they will think that I am a little kid. When I get out of here, they will still treat me as such. I don't want that.

I want to be off on my own. Well anyway, so much for the family problems.

Now that you have read this letter, you can stop worrying yourself. I am alright. I didn't get hurt. Tomorrow, I go up to see the old man. When I do, I'll let you know what happens to me. Whatever that he gives to me will not be as bad as the ribbing I got from the boys. They called me a jailbird and all the other names that goes with them.

Well, Baby, that is about all in this letter. Be sweet, will you, Baby? I love you so much. I love you, I love you, I love you, I love you, Baby.

You were looking for a name for me; now you have one, Jailbird.

Yours,
Elijah "Jailbird" Porter

July 10, 1952

Dearest Darling,

After reading your letter, I just had to answer it before tomorrow.

When you said you didn't make it easy for me, you only said part of it. It was like trying to walk through a fire barefoot; you really sent something moving inside of me. I did not feel too well. How can I tell you how I felt when you were feeling the same way? Margaret, all I know is that I love you no matter; that's all that matters to me. My feelings were hurt deeply that night. And the next day, if you felt like did you know only I am sorry that what happened made you cry. You seemed so much like a little baby to me; that is all you are. But you are the most effective baby I know.

Margaret, I know you didn't give me the wrong impression of you under the circumstances. Most any girl would have acted the same as you did, and any boy would have been happy except me. I was and wasn't. I wanted to jump at this chance but didn't. Sometimes, my emotions run away, but I get them back under control. Margaret, I want you for who you are, not because of the little pleasure you can give to me for a few minutes. After those minutes, there isn't anything else. I want you always, not just for enjoyment. I want you as my wife, and the only way I can get you is to be nice and be myself. If I let all feelings and what I would like to do go away, you would not love me as you say you do.

You said you love me, and I believe you. Honest, I do. What people say do not bother me at all. It is you I want, not the public. They just like to talk because they have nothing else to do. So what if they talk? As long as you are happy, then so am I. When you are unhappy, I am too. You are a part of me deep down inside. You don't have to wait forever for me. I am only asking you to wait three more years. You want a church wedding? Well, so do I. Whatever you want is what I want. I know who you are even if I have only kissed you. You are the girl I love. If I did have sex with you, it would make you feel that was all I wanted from you. I know that we have had lots of chances, but we turned them all down. I think that we know what we are doing, and it is all for the best. Most girls think that's what all boys want. Well, Margaret, I don't want you to think that of me. Sure, I am just like the next fellow, but I think about the future.

I never want to help bring a kid into the world without a name or a place to live. I want my kids to know who their mother and father is. I never want them or you to have to pretend about their father or your husband. This has been going on since the beginning of time. You and I have waited this long, and I can wait until I get out. I have waited this long, so another few years won't matter as long as I have you. That's all that I worry about and think of all the time. All I want is Margaret Williams because with you, I am something; without you, I am nothing.

Well, I must close now. My first day back and I get a mid-watch. Well, that's Navy life for you. I will write again tomorrow if I can and tell you what the Captain did to me. I love you, Baby.

Yours always,
Elijah Porter

July 12, 1952

Dearest Darling,

I started to write this letter yesterday but gave up until today. Well, I was up to see the Captain. That was something. There were six other fellows up there with me. I wasn't afraid much, just enough to want to get it over with. The fellows before me got 14 days restriction and extra duty. When my time came around to step up, I got a big lump in my throat. It left as fast as it came. I explained why I was late and all that, but he still chewed me up a little. One of the officers took a little off me by telling him I was a good little boy. The old man must have been feeling good as he only gave me three days extra duty and a good talking too. I don't think that I will have to go to see him again; once was enough. I worked off my extra duty by marching around the ship. I think I am in the army, what a thought. Well anyway, that's over now, and I can go back to work. I sure got a name out of it. Now all the fellows call me a jailbird; what a name. That is worse than the one I have now.

Margaret, last night, some of the fellows were kidding me about you. I had your letters out, so they got your address. If you get any mail from them, don't believe a word that they say. They are always doing something like that. Besides, they are real nice fellows once you get to know them. I hope that you don't.

Well, Baby, that about takes care of all the news for now. When some more occur, I'll cut you in on the scoop.

Yours,
Elijah Porter

July 14, 1952

Dearest Darling,

I had to answer this letter tonight before finally going to bed.

I am sorry if I hurt your feelings by crying, but if you had seen me walk away as I saw you walk away, I am positive that you would have cried too.

I am very glad that you really want me for who I am and not for what I can give to you for a few minutes. Also, I am glad that you want me for your wife because you could have picked anyone.

Elijah, you said that you only want me to wait for three more years. I will try my best to wait and to make them worth waiting for because I love you so much. Until I am willing to wait as long as we both are sure that we want each other as much as we say. If we find out that we don't want to wait that long and still be together, then we can always change our minds and go our separate ways.

I know that I am lucky to have a person like you, because you can count the boys on your finger that will take your word for what you say. I couldn't ask for a more sweeter or nicer person than you. Thanks a lot for being understandable and loveable as you are.

I love you now and always will.

Your loving sweetheart,
Margaret

July 19, 1952

Dearest Darling,

Before I answer your other letter, I thought this one should be answered first. They found me in the best of health. After being down, they brought me up. I was feeling pretty low about a lot of things. I guess that I think too hard about you and my family. I can't seem to comprehend the problems of my family. Maybe I am trying to settle everything with them, and I can't. I wish that I was there to talk to you, as you seem to understand better than other people. Why is it like this when I want you the most? We are so far apart. This is a time when a man needs somebody to talk to beside other men. I mean, a person he loves and understands him. Things have a way of coming out right. I can always help other people with their troubles but never my own. After I write to you, I feel a whole lot better. Right now, I don't think there is much of anything that could cheer me other than you.

Margaret, it wasn't your fault that I was late. I would have been anyway. I had a feeling that I was going to be late before leaving, so you don't have to feel bad about that. I don't, so you shouldn't I just feel upset about everything concerning my family.

When I said that we had an accident, I didn't mean to express it that way. We just lost two tires off the port side; that was all.

Remember you are marrying me and not my family.

Well, this about all in this letter. I'll answer the other one because it calls for my best answers. Be sweet will you; I still love you, Baby.

I love you, I love you, I love you, I love you, I love you, I love you, I love you now and always. Is that enough proof?

Yours always,
Elijah Porter

August 14, 1952

Hi Margaret,

While dreaming of you, I thought that I should write to you now that the excitement is over. Saturday night, we had a basketball game up here. We won this one, 61 to 38, and who do you think had the second highest score? Yours truly, Elijah Seaman Recruit Porter, with 19 points. The first guy had 24 points, and the rest had below the 10 margin. I also played 60 minutes; that was Saturday.

Yesterday, we had another victory for this company. I wanted to write you last night, but I didn't get back to the barracks until eleven o'clock, and then I didn't feel like doing anything but to sleep. The reason is as follows. Every week, some unlucky person in this company has to box. Well, this week was my unlucky week. I don't know how I did it but, Margaret, I won in the third round. The first two rounds in that ring were awfully hot ones. When I went in there, I forgot about everybody and everything. The only thing that was on my mind was that big 158-lb guy and his big 7-ounce gloves; I only weighed 148 lbs. The faster I gained weight, I lose it back on Saturday and Sunday. Those are the sporting days, and I try to take part in every one, even those that I lose. If you think boxing is easy, try it sometime (smile), but make sure you can beat your opponent (smile). Not me, I don't fight girls especially someone as nice and in love like you are. I hope you don't think that I am a show off because I am not. Margaret, please don't tell my mother about the fights because I wouldn't want her to worry. I am a big boy now and can take care of myself. I don't want you to worry neither. I didn't get hurt too much. I only have a swollen eye and lip, so you really don't have to worry about me.

Margaret, if my mother knew too much about me, she would start feeling kind of funny if you told her what I am telling you and you alone. Don't think I am trying to sound like somebody who is trying to make another person cry by telling you the truth I have finally found myself.

I said that I was going to give you a ring for your graduation. Well, something new has been added after I leave here. I am to go to sea for how long. I don't know where I'm to be stationed. Well, here is the problem. If you would like, I could give it to you on my 14 days home or send it to you when you graduate if I couldn't be home in person to give it to you.

Margaret don't think I am only giving it to you because I think it's right. I know it's right. I wouldn't want to look at another girl if I couldn't look at you. I miss you so much now that I take your picture out of my wallet and just stare at you.

Margaret, I have plenty of time to think, and I know that you are the only girl for me. It seems like we were supposed to be together for now and always. Please write me back and tell me what to do. I know I have to ask your mother and father first. Well, I can. Which way would you like for me to ask them? Personally, I would like to ask them in person. Then, maybe, they wouldn't think that I was too afraid to ask them like a man.

Write me and tell me what way, how and when you want me to ask them and when you would like for me to give you the ring, and your finger measurements and kind of ring. Be nice and answer me soon so I can let myself know that I am doing the right things.

Well, I must check in now.

Yours until the end of time,
Elijah Porter

September 11, 1952

Dearest Darling,

Before we leave for Puerto Rico, I thought I would write you because I don't know when I will be able to write again for we will be gone for a few months. If you do not hear from me soon, don't think there is anything the matter with me or I have forgotten you. I haven't.

Margaret, I am sorry that I gave you the wrong idea about buying me something. When a fellow takes a girl out, he likes to show off his best girl. He does things to make her happy. If she is nice, as you are, he doesn't mind. I like to show you off because it makes me feel awful good inside to see you smiling and being happy.

I don't need anything, so you do not have to worry about me wanting anything. You have given me more than enough already. Anybody would be happy with that; your love is all that I ask and that is enough for me. I understand why you can't take a chance on other things, so don't worry about satisfying me. It doesn't take much to make me happy. Just being with you and holding you in my arms is the most wonderful feeling in the world. I do love you, Margaret. I love you more than anything else in the whole world. It is something that grows and grows, and then comes out when I come home to you. That is what makes me come back. Don't ask me why, but if you were not waiting for me, there wouldn't be a very good reason for coming back home.

Sure, I know I have a family. Everybody does; some of that is different. I need someone to come back to beside them. They can't give me the enjoyment that you give to me when I am feeling bad or have something on my mind, and my mother does not understand as you do. She understands a little, but not like you. I can't feel like a king when I talk to them all together.

Margaret, you mean a whole lot to me no matter how many ports I hit and how many girls I meet; none of them can take your place. They just don't have a chance at all. It is a one-party line for me. Most girls think sailors have a girl in every port. Some do, I can answer that question truthfully; I don't. Only in one port, and that is where ever you are.

We see a lot of pretty women, but it's you who I love and care for. Let someone else worry about them; I like to worry about you.

Well, that is about all for now. I got to hit my sack. I'll be seeing you, Baby. I love I love you I love you, Margaret. I am yours.

Elijah Porter

September 18, 1952

Dearest Darling,

As I sit here thinking of you tonight and wishing you were near, my heart and soul seem to say I am yours. It seems like years since we saw each other. It could be longer, for I want to be near you now and hold you in my arms, then I wouldn't feel so blue on a night like this. There are no sounds except the wind and the vibration of the ship outside. It is so dark, like a piece of blue and black sky. One seems to remind me of you. They are saying, "Don't worry, Elijah. Margaret loves you as she says that she does, and if you keep loving her as you have, you will make her a very happy wife. For it is only a few hundred that can find a sweeter girl." Each one of them seems to spell out your name. All the little ones are saying something very sweet about you. Me, all I can do is think, hope, wish and pray. This night, and nights like this, makes me feel like I was never meant to be a sailor; you do too darn much thinking about a girl and what I would like to do when my time is up.

Margaret, I have told you that I love you. Well, I am telling you again so that you won't forget. I know you won't, but just to make you think about me a little more, I am saying it again. I love you, Baby. I love you so much that I can't find any other words to say except "I love you, Margaret, with all my heart." Baby, I am crazy as can be. One hundred and ninety-nine percent crazy about you. How can a girl like you make a guy like me fall so much in love that he stays awake half the night, dreaming pretty things about you? Why is it that I love you so? It is because you are the girl I love; the only girl I will ever love no matter what. This, I can promise you. I am yours, and Baby, I want to remain yours for eternity.

There isn't much more to say. It is getting me to feel kind of blue and wandering away from what I should be doing. Thinking about you takes up all of my time. After that, there isn't anything else to do.

Well, Margaret, Baby, I guess I will turn in now. So long, Baby.

Yours,
Elijah Willie Lump, Lump Porter

Mighty, Angel, Royal, Guicy, Armful, Religious, Easy, Temper—this is Margaret.

Willing, Intoxicating, Lovely, Loyal, In my Heart, Always Sweet, Mine, Sweet—this is Williams.

September 23, 1952

Dearest Darling,

While sitting down, I thought I would write you a letter and to see how you are, and also to tell you the latest news.

I didn't get any wrong ideas about my buying you something because I think that the least I can do is to buy you a birthday present when you come home. You spend all of your money on me. Can't I show you my appreciation by buying you something now and then instead of appearing as a person who wants everything for herself and nothing for anyone else?

You never have to be jealous of any other fellows that may be around me because they don't mean anything to me other than as friends.

I love you and is wearing your ring, not theirs. The next time that you see anyone that you feel that you don't want around me, then you should tell them.

Now for the real news, Mattie's girlfriend put out news that I am pregnant that is why we got engaged. I told Mattie to tell her that I was and if she was going to pay my doctor bill. So when you come home again, they will tell you that you are going to become a father and you won't be surprised. I can't believe that people know more about what is going on with us than we do. I have no idea of how I could get pregnant when you are only kissing me (smile).

I am so lonesome without you until I don't know what to do. I wish that you were here to hold me in your arms and to kiss away all of my loneliness. We still have a little less than two years before we can be together all the time and not have to worry as to when we can see each other.

Write to you again soon.

Love you as always,
Margaret

November 2, 1952

Dearest Darling,

I received your letter and was very glad to hear from you. I am fine and hope when you receive this letter, you will be the same. I told you before that I wanted to go New York, to my cousin's wedding, and I didn't know that was on the 25th of October. I left on Friday night and came back Sunday night. I had a wonderful time. She had a big wedding at the church and a reception to follow. She also had a four-room apartment, all furnished and ready to move into when she comes back from her honeymoon.

All the boys were crazy about me and didn't want me to come home (smile).

I received the pictures, and they were very nice. I took them over to your house and showed them to your family; they liked them very much.

Elijah, I miss you so much until I don't know what to do. I am so lonesome on the weekends until when I went away last weekend and was out with other girls and boys that I really enjoyed myself and wished that it all didn't have to end so soon. That's what happens to you when you are lonely and no one to go out with.

I will never really be happy until we are together for good and to be with each other. Then we can do all things that we would have done if you didn't join the Navy.

Since I saw my cousin's wedding, I am convinced that I do want a church wedding.

Write soon.

Love,
Margaret

November 5, 1952

Dearest Darling,

There isn't much of anything going on so I thought I would write you. I am fine and hope that when you receive this letter, it will find you in the best of everything.

Today we left a very nice port down in *Ciudad Trujillo*; we spent four days there. We could have stayed longer, but the old man (Captain) couldn't see it. I think I'll trade this port in for Cuba.

It was much nicer than any place I have been since I have been in the Navy. Just like State side, the people are mostly all colored. I wouldn't call them colored because they are so mixed up. Spanish and German are the language spoken down here. They talk too fast to understand any of it. This time, there wasn't many sailors around either. So we really had a wonderful time.

Margaret, Baby, what am I going to do with you? You seem so far away yet so near to me. I can't sleep anymore for thinking of you and wondering if you are alright. I don't know why I always seem to think something is the matter. I try to throw that idea away, but it keeps coming back; so try and take care of yourself so nothing will happen to you. If something did, I would be hurt deeply. For if maybe I was there, it wouldn't have been as bad as it is when I am away. Some of my dreams are crazy. In the middle of the night, I wake up calling you. Now you see why single beds have to go (smile)? I even look for you in my dreams. Just think how it would be in a bed myself (smile)? You can never guess how much effect you have on my life, but it is all yours as well as my heart and soul. You take them; I'll never use them, as you have them. If there were ever a lucky guy in this world, I think I am him. Lucky because I have such a wonderful girl as you. Someday soon, I would like to change that girl into a wife. I think she would make as good a mother as she did as a girlfriend. She is what I want or ever will want, just her and all her love now and forever. She has all my love and that she doesn't have is being saved until I see you again. Then I can hold you in my arms and never let you go.

Bye now, Baby. I still love you, honey

Yours always,
Elijah (Crazy) Porter

November 8, 1952

Dearest Darling,

I received your letter a few days ago and was so thrilled to hear from you that I didn't know what to do.

I am fine and hope when you receive this letter, you will be in the best of health.

You said in your letter why did a sweet little girl like me get mixed with you. If I didn't enjoy being mixed with you, don't you think that I would have stopped this before we got this far, engaged and awaiting for you this long? I have told you that I love you and no one else, but you don't seem to believe me.

Only one thing, I can't help but to blame you for all the loneliness that you are causing me by being in the Navy. Like tonight, Billy Eckstine, George Shearing and Count Basie are at the Mosque Theater; but where am I? At home. Why? Because my big, handsome, future husband decided that he wanted to join the Navy. Well, it is done now, and neither one of us can help it if I get too lonely.

This is the price that I have to pay for falling in love with you and getting engaged. I will never cheat on you.

I love you.

Your Darling,
Margaret

December 8, 1952

Dearest Darling,

You must be wondering why I haven't written to you in a long time. Well, I wanted to, but my deal didn't come true. I was planning on coming up there last weekend and coming up there this weekend too. My boys went on leave before I could get away; now we are a little shorthanded.

My leave will start the 28th of December and end the 5th of January, so you see, we won't have to wait long to be together. A little time is better than none at all, isn't it?

Sherman and I had a deal cooking, but it ran away because he will not be able to come home soon. All of my deals didn't pan out. I said my leave starts the 28th, but if some of the fellows come back before then, maybe I can get off that Friday. I won't know until then. I know I'll be home before next year. My hope is built on that for I want to see you so much.

Margaret, if I bring that package home after Christmas instead of sending it, will it be alright? I was going to send it, but I thought I was going to come up last week but didn't. Now I'll keep you in suspense until then (smile). I hope you don't have me in suspense so both of us can't pull the same deal.

This is about all for now. Bye. I will be looking to seeing you soon.

Yours only,
Elijah Porter, Here to Stay

December 19, 1952

Dearest Darling,

When you receive this letter, I hope it will find you very happy and looking forward to a Merry Christmas and a very happy New Year.

The reason I haven't written is because I am kind of busy. Most of the cooks are on leave, and only four of us are aboard to cook for the crew. Don't be angry at me for not writing as often as other fellows write to their girls. I still love you, Margaret, no matter how long we are apart. Even if I die, I know something is between us that will never die.

Two years ago, today, you went south and left one of the loneliest boy in the world. I thought I would never be that lonely again, but today, I feel twice as lonely. Margaret, I miss you now more than ever. I keep seeing you and can't be with you. Maybe it is because I'll be home next weekend and can't hardly wait until then. Whatever it is, I want it to stay this way. I feel lonely and restless every minute of the day. If I didn't have you, I wouldn't feel a thing. I am glad I have you, someone to love as I love you. That is more than any man can ask for.

Now Christmas is here again, and I can't spend it with you. It seems we will never be able to spend Christmas together until we get married. Then maybe we can make up for all the ones we missed.

This is about all for now. I would like to wish you a very Merry Christmas, a wonderful New Year. I can't be there for Christmas, but I will be there for New Year.

Be sweet until then. I love you, my darling, even if I don't write you as often as I should.

Yours always,
Elijah Porter

A Santa Claus face was in a drawing.
Wishing you and all your family a Merry Xmas and a Happy New Year

From,
Willie Lump Lump & Company
6

---

6 This was a funny nickname that Elijah would use at times.

Letters and Pictures (1953)

Dear Darling,

Thinking tonight of you so much that I just had to write you. I hope you have gotten over your colds by now. When I was home on seven days leave, I lost ten pounds. Just think of how much weight I would have lost if I had more leave. It would not of, mattered if I could be with you.

Now it seems like it will be a long time before we see each other again. When I was home, I wanted to tell you something, Margaret, but couldn't. I kept seeing you smile, and I couldn't tell you. You see, after we leave Charleston in March, we are going to the West Coast for duty.

I don't know how long we will be over there. That is something unknown. I know I can't be over there no more than two and a half years. If I never see you again until my time is up, Margaret, remember this. No matter how far I am away or how long I am away from you, I love you only. If I do stay away for a long time, you are the only girl I could ever love like I do.

I am sorry that I have to tell you this in a letter, but that is the way it goes.

If people do tell you a lot of stories about us sailors, believe this, I am your sailor boy. And no girl in the whole world can take me from you, no matter what she has or how pretty she is. I love you so much that nothing else matters to me as long as you are happy.

Maybe we will be back in Norfolk before we go, I don't know. All I know is that I love you with all my heart. If we do, I'll try to come home on a weekend to see you. I really don't know if I can or not. I might not be able to make it from Charleston on a weekend as transportation is very bad from down here.

Margaret, I worry about losing you all the time. That is what was on my mind when you saw me looking sick. I am so in love with you that I just can't lose you now. You said that I had nothing to worry about, but I still worry anyway. Even if you didn't tell me, I would still worry. I stay away from you so much that I can't help but to worry about it.

When I see you, I try to make up for all the time that I have been away. I like to kiss you all the time because that is the only thing I can do to keep myself from overflowing with tears. I may not make the best husband, or the nicest, but I think I could make you a very happy person. When all of this is over with, then we can start out on our own. It is hard on you waiting for me all the time. I understand a whole lot better now than I did before, but most of all, I understand you now. Maybe because I have gotten a little older, and maybe because I am getting to be a man(smile). Whatever it is, I love it.

No man in the whole world has ever loved a person as I love you, so be sweet for me, Baby.

Elijah Porter

January 14, 1953

Dearest Darling,

Your lovely letter found me in deep meditation. I was thinking about you while lying in my sack when the mail came. This letter of yours completed my thoughts.

Since I got back on time, we didn't stop until we got back to Norfolk. We pulled into the Greyhound Station at 0600, so I had two hours to get back to the ship. Don't worry about me so much; I'll be OK.

No, Margaret, I don't think you are doing something that I would disapprove of. You are old enough to know what you want to do. I can't tell you what to do and what not to do; that is something you have to figure out for yourself. All I want you to do is to be happy and keep on loving me as you have. That is all I ask of you for the present. Later on, I can tell you what to do to a certain point. Then I won't tell you much. I have told you before, I didn't like telling people what to do. I just don't like to give orders to anybody. I am sorry if you like for me to be that way, but that is not the way I am.

I never want to go any place because as long as I am with you, I am happy. Only when I am with you, the days seem to be shorter. Maybe I try to put too much in twenty-four hours. That is the only way to try and make up for lost time, which can never be made up no matter how hard I try. These four years will always be lost to me all the time. I want to talk to you about anything that come up, anything. As long as I am talking to you, then I see you. I can't find the words to say; that is why I am so quiet. You must think I am kind of crazy all the time. I write about wanting to talk to you, then when I have a chance, I don't say nothing. If you could see into my heart, you would know what is going on inside of me. All the time, I just want to be near you. Even if it is just to sit and look at you, that is enough for me. It is like looking at a merry-go-round; I get dizzy looking at you. My mind seem to wander and think of things, just sweet, lovely things which has no interest to no one except me.

I didn't mind you writing in pencil. You could write in water, and it would be OK with me. All I care about is hearing from you.

So long for now.

Love always,
Elijah Porter

January 17, 1953

Dearest Darling,

I received your most adorable letters and was very glad to hear from you. I am fine and hope when you receive this letter, you will be fine also.

You asked why did I disappear so fast at the station. Josh was ready to leave. He was going to take me home and he didn't want to wait any longer, so I had to leave too if I wanted to go home with him. You know that I wouldn't have gone so fast otherwise.

Why do you keep worrying about losing me because you stay away from me so much? I told you a dozen times that you don't have to worry about me leaving you. I am engaged to you, I want you to be my husband, and you can't be it if you lose me; so why don't you stop worrying before you lose all of your hair (smile)?

Don't you know that other boys don't want girls that are engaged to be married? Then they think that they might get hurt if they bother with them because they might fall in love with them and she not with them, so you really do not have anything to worry about. It is just your imagination that is bothering you.

My mother and father received your letter too and were very glad to hear from you, but as you know that they don't answer letters. They send their love to you, and I think that they care as much for you as you do for them.

I wrote Sherman a letter last night while at school. I have only four more weeks, and I will be finished with school at least for a while.

I am at work, so I will close now.

Love you as always,
Margaret

February 4, 1953

Dearest Elijah,

I received your letter a few days ago, and it found me in the best of health. And I hope when you receive this letter, you will be fine also.

Everybody is doing fine in both of the families. You remember that I told you that your mother and father was going to Agnes's uncle's wedding? Well, they did go, and your father got high and promised that he wasn't going to another wedding ever, not even to his own children's. I don't believe it, do you?

I received a letter from your friend Warren the same day that I received your letter, and he said that you told him that I had told you to tell him hello when you were home the last time, which seems like years ago (smile). He also told me that he wanted a picture of me because he sent me one of him, but I don't have any pictures of myself, so you can give him one of yours (smile).

When have you heard from Sherman last, how is he? I think that he wrote to me last and that I owe him a letter, but I am not sure.

The weather here is very cold, and everybody has colds. Quite a few of the people on my job is out or has been out due to colds.

Sunday is my birthday, and how I wish that you were here to help me celebrate it. I want to go to New York, but I am not sure whether I will or not. I want to see a Broadway show, but they don't show them on Sundays, and the whole family wanted to go. Then I was going to get tickets for the day before my birthday, but Catherine said that the tickets cost too much. They were $4.80 a piece, but I was willing to pay for them because I wanted to see the show very badly since I had heard so much about it. The name of the show is "Wish You Were Here." Maybe I will go to New York anyway, only to a different movie or to the Apollo or someplace like that. Any place that I go, it won't be the same as if I went with you.

Believe it or not, the time is really passing fast to me, how is it with you? Do you realize that this is the second month of the year already? If only the rest of the months and years would go this fast, then we would be together that much sooner. I will close now, I am at work, all alone in my office, so I decided that now was a good time to drop you a few lines.

I love you even if you don't believe me. I really don't believe that you don't believe that I love you. Do you think that your love is a one-sided affair (smile)? Well, it isn't. I love you as much as you love me. Maybe I don't say it as much as you do, but that doesn't mean that I don't because I do. How many times do you want me to say it?

I love you, I love you, I love you, I love you, I love you. Is that enough times? If not, I will tell you until you think that it is enough.

I am still going to the dentist. Saturday past, he filled one of my teeth, and it didn't hurt when he was grinding and drilling it before he filled it. I have to go again tomorrow and maybe he will fill another one. When he does the front, I know that it is going to hurt, and I can't wait until this is all over with.

I will close now. See you in my dreams. Love You.

Margaret

February 14, 1953

Dear Valentine,

Your most adorable card made me a very happy receiver. It was something that I will always remember. Not for this Valentine Day, but all Valentine Days to come. It said things I couldn't say, and some of them are true and some are not. Let the ones that are true be remembered, and the ones false be forgotten.

I love you on this day like all other days; but, honey, on this day, I love you a little more because February is a month where all good things happened to me. The best one was finding you. If all of my February's keep being like this one, then this will be my favorite month as years go by. I will always remember this month, you and all the things that it holds so dear to my heart. February, keep smiling and make a little girl's heart smile back at you, for I love her much, too much to lose her now.

Be sweet, baby, and keep smiling.

Yours,
E. Porter
[7]

---

[7] February kept smiling. On February 8, 1964, a son named Mark was born to Elijah and Margaret on Margaret's birthday, February 8.

February 15, 1953

Dearest Darling,

I received your beautiful card yesterday and was more than glad to receive it. Some girls get candy and all kinds of things, but to me, the one Valentine card meant more than five boxes of candy all put together. You'll never know how much it really did mean to me. Thank you ever so much, and I will be your Valentine as long as you want me to. I thought at first that you had forgotten me and wouldn't ever send me a card, but you did remember, and that is what counts.

I also received your letters, and they found me well. I hope that you are well too. I am glad that you called me on my birthday because it shows that you think of me.

You said maybe I got the wrong idea when you said that you could stay out all night. I didn't because I trust you, and I hope that you trust me. I don't care what you do as long as you don't do anything that will hurt the two of us. You asked me if I am sorry that you are in love with me, the answer is no. Only, there is one thing. I don't want you to love me so much as to make yourself look like a fool, and people start talking about you. I wouldn't want a better person to love me than you because you are the one that I love, and I want you to love me too. There is one thing that I don't like you to call me and that is "baby" because it sounds to me as if you are trying to say that I am a young baby.

Elijah, my mother and I were talking the other night, and she said that when we get married, we could have the whole first floor of their house, which would be four rooms, and leaving an extra room for my grandmother for when she comes to visit. In other words, we could have a big bedroom, living room, kitchen and a spare bedroom for company or something until we get ready to buy a home of our own. We could then pay them so much a month for the apartment and buy the very best of furniture that we would want in our own home. When we move, there would be much less furniture that we would have to buy. I was thinking that if we both saved our money, we could pay at least half down on the furniture, and then a year or two later. After it is paid for and we have saved more money, we could buy our own home.

I think this is a good idea because it still isn't the same as living in the same apartment with them. We will be on the first floor, and there will not be any confusion, but it is up to you. I wouldn't consent to doing anything unless you approve, and please don't approve just to make me happy because I want you to be happy also. If you like or dislike this suggestion, please tell me. Don't lie about it because in the end, we both will get hurt. Do think it over before answering.

When you get out, I want you to get a job and get settled back into normal life. Then we will plan a wedding. And if you see fit for us to have a honeymoon, we will; and if you don't, you can tell me. I won't get angry because I want us to get ahead as soon as possible so that we can relax with ease and then have children. Let us not plan on children right away, at least until we have gotten something to show of our marriage first. I am saving as much as possible. I am saving each week out of my paycheck for saving bonds. Also, I am saving through the Christmas club which will be put in the bank at the end of the year. So you see, I am trying to help you prepare for our future, so please try to help me too; and in that way, we can make up for the lost time which we have had.

I love you and you love me. Now is the time to think about our future so that when you do come home, we will not have to waste time thinking about should we do this or should we do that. Please answer right away if you agree with me or not. Also, help me if your ideas are different from mine.

Elijah, there is one thing I want you to do. That is, if you see any beautiful dishes over there, get a set for us so that we will have them later. After I get my dentist's bill and everything paid,

I am saving my money and buying things that we will need in the future.

I will close now. Don't forget to think over everything that I have told you.

Love,
Margaret

February 22, 1953

Dearest Darling,

When you receive this letter, I hope it will find you as happy and cheerful as yours found me. You said that you wanted me to answer right away, but I had to do a little more thinking before I answered your letter this time. It was nice to hear you liked your Valentine card. I tried to send it so that you would get it on the 14th of February, and I have not forgotten you even if I am late when holidays do come around. I think about you all the time, so how could I forget someone as sweet as you are. I love you, and if people do start to talk, let them. Loving you will never be too much. If you keep being nice and treat me right, I will always love you no matter what you do or think as long as you be sweet to me as you have been. You won't have to worry about me or the future.

Don't get upset if I call you baby; that is all I can call you. It is not that you are a young baby; it is just that you are my baby and no one else. I wanted a nickname to call you, and baby seems to fit you, so I call you baby. You are my baby, so let me keep calling you that until I can find another name for you, OK?

Margaret, before I came into the Navy, I knew what I wanted to do. That is to save as much money as I could. So I took bonds to be able to save. My future was planned when I first met you. I knew I could never get what I wanted if I worked at Issies, in the grocery store, for twenty years. So I joined the Navy on a chance that if I got in, I could save my money; so when I go out, I would have enough of my own to start a life with you. Now I am in here. I have kept what is true. Since the way that we feel toward each other now, I think we will be very happy when we get married. It seems like we both want the same things and like to do the same things. That is why we get along so well. I always wanted a church wedding, and I sure would like to be married in style the first time because there won't be a second time for me.

I know it will take me a few months to get back to normal life, but if you are there, it will not be too bad. You may think I haven't changed, but I have. Only you never see me long enough to find out how much. It is a thing that changes a person's ways and actions when they are in the service.

We don't have to have children right away, but that won't stop the other thing, will it? (smile) Later, after we get settled, then we can have a few kids. That is OK as long as you are the mother of them. What I would like to do is don't wait too long after I get out to get married, about two or three months after, or the sooner the better.

When we get over to California, I will try to get some dishes. We are still down here in Charleston, and they don't have anything down here. If we get any liberty on the West Coast, I will get a set of dishes for you (us). They won't cost much because I have connections with some people out there (Uncle Sam).

I'll close now.

Yours,
Elijah Porter

February 26, 1953

Dearest Darling,

Three years ago tonight, I never thought that I would be doing this, but here I am writing you a letter three years later. That is how things are. If someone had told me that I was going to fall in love with you, then it would be a mystery for I didn't know what this thing was. Now that I have fallen so deeply in love with you, I am happy. It has been a long time since we said yes to each other. Only I didn't know what your answer would be when I asked you if you wanted a boyfriend, so it was hard on me to ask you. Something just made me ask you and you said yes, then we kissed. Now look at me. I am here all alone to celebrate a thing like this. If you were here, it would be altogether different. I know it would because whenever I am with you, it is like being in heaven.

Come to think of it, I have broken a few records. I have broken a few records in three years. We have not had intercourse yet. I had some chances but never did. It won't be like that next time. I want to know how you would react. The only way I can tell is to try and find out (smile). It would be nice to find out. Most boys don't wait this long to find out, but it is worth waiting for if they had something and someone worth waiting for. If I come home on a good date (smile) next time and we can be alone, how about it? Answer back real fast.

I know you think I am a fresh boy, don't you? Let me tell you something. I know you are afraid of getting pregnant; I won't do that for nothing not at least until we are married. You told me before to wait until then, but I still got two years to go before I get out. I may not see you until then. If I don't see you until then, you have nothing to worry about; but if I do, you will)smile). I have waited for three years to find out how you would react, so don't you think it is about time to find out?

Margaret, don't get me wrong. I was thinking about this, and this is what was on my mind. You can't fault me, can you (smile)? What else is there to think about than being in someone's arms such as yours?

Be sweet and take care of yourself, Baby

Yours,
Elijah Porter

March 3, 1953

Dearest Elijah,

I received your letter and very sorry to say that for the first time, I wasn't pleased to hear from you, especially when you talk like you were talking in my last letter. You said that you love me. Well, after that last letter, I really wonder whether you do or not. You said that you have broken a few records. Well, if you don't watch your step, I am going to do a little breaking, and it won't be in records either; it will be our engagement. You said that we are going to have intercourse the next time you come home, and I say no. You also said that I am afraid of becoming pregnant, well, maybe I am, but I also like people talking about me the way I am now. I haven't had a baby up until now, and I don't intend to have one any time soon even if it means our friendship has to end.

Having just heard of a person having another baby had upset me very much, and I am a nervous wreck from it as she is a very close friend. I don't expect it to happen to me just to please some other person. I love you, but I am afraid that I don't love you enough to have people pointing a finger at me, saying that I had a child out of wedlock. If you won't wait until we are married, then I am sorry because I don't intend on doing anything that will hurt me later.

It is hard for me to wait too, but I have to; and if you can't, please let me know. I am sorry that this came up, but since it has, it is better because in this way, we know where we stand with each other. And if you aren't willing to wait, I think that we had better call off our marriage. That is how much it means to me, and if you love me, you will wait like I am waiting for you to come home to be my husband.

Please don't think I am mean or anything, but you better be glad that you weren't near me when I read this letter because I think that you would now be without a girlfriend. If you had mentioned this to me before I heard about this friend, maybe we could talk about it in a more calmly fashion, but I was furious. We have been together for three years, and you and I have always been in agreement as to when we were going to have sex, and then you write this kind of letter to me. I am nineteen years old and feel that sex before marriage is not for me.

I still love you; don't think that I don't because I do. But please let's be patient a while longer.

I am looking forward to an answer soon.

Love,
Margaret

March 6, 1953

Dearest,

When you receive this letter, we will be at sea again because in a few days, we will leave Charleston S.C. I hope this letter will do a great deal of good for my side. You had a very good reason for writing me as you did, only I never wanted a letter from you like that. If I hadn't said those foolish things, maybe I never would have gotten one; but I did, and what it did to me was something I'll never get over for a long time. Now I know how other fellows feel. I love you deeply even if sometimes I sound as if I don't, and I really hope we don't have to break up because I didn't mean all the things I said before. Why I said them, I don't know. I thought I was smart or something but wasn't at all.

There is not much that I can ask you except to forgive me for I don't want to lose you. That is what I have always disliked and never wanted to happen; but me and my bright ideas seem to always mess up things. I never want to hurt or do anything that would hurt you, so it seems that I have hurt you deeply, and now I want to ask you to forgive me for something I said. What I said will never happen until we get married because I don't want it too. Whenever I talk like I did before, it wasn't meant to sound as it did. It sounded the wrong way. I can wait as long as you want me to, and it would be better off later than now.

Most of all, I don't want our friendship to end. Not now, or at any time. All I know is I love you now. I feel awful lonely. I feel like a person left on an island by himself with nothing to do but think and think all because of the bad letter sent to someone who means a whole lot to me. If it is up to me, you will never get married by a shotgun wedding.

I am going to ask you this, and it may sound stupid, but will you still wait for me and forgive me for saying what I did. I will never bring it up again. If you leave me now, there wouldn't be anything for me left in this world that I could come back to. It sounds foolish, but it is true. For you mean that much to me and more than I'll ever be able to tell you. Sure, there are other girls, but not like you or will ever be like you for me. I would never be the same without you.

I love you and I can wait a long time, and I don't think you are mean or anything like that. It was my fault for trying to be wise; now it hurts, and I don't like the way in which it feels.

Margaret, I am sorry that I can't write more and tell you how much you mean to me, but it is hard for me to write. Now I am afraid that I would sound wrong. I just can't write anymore right now.

Please forgive me; that is what I am asking you. I would have answered your letter yesterday but couldn't write a line. I love you, and I don't want to break up with you even if I sound crazy sometimes. I will try to write more next time, but we won't hit any land until March 16th. After that, we will be out on the water all of the time, then over to the West Coast.

I can wait, and I understand how you feel. Maybe this letter will make you feel better, and maybe it won't. I hope it does for it means a whole lifetime to me; I'll close for now.

Yours,
E. Porter

March 9, 1953

Dearest Darling,

I received your letter, and this time, I am very happy to say that I enjoyed receiving it. It was just what I wanted to hear. It makes me feel so much better as you hoped it would. You think that you were suffering; believe me, I was suffering just as bad as you.

I thought maybe you would take me up on what I said, and you would say let's break up, but you didn't. I have never felt more that I love you, and your love for me. When it came to a point that we might lose each other, we both felt bad about it; that's proof enough.

I hope you don't worry too long about it. It was something that has happened, and maybe it was for the best. You don't have to worry; we won't break up now or ever.

There is nothing really for me to forgive you for I should be the one to ask forgiveness, as for I am the one who said all the mean things which really caused the trouble. We can forgive each other.

What you asked me, you can ask me again; but make sure when you do, that you are home and know how I feel and what is going on. I don't blame you for asking me. After all, you are human and how much do I think you can take. You require sex as much as the next person, and if it makes you feel any better, ask me. I can always say no if I feel that I shouldn't do it.

Don't feel lonely, as you said you do, because I am still yours like I have been in the past; and I still love you even more. You asked me, will I wait for you? I will for you, for another two years, plus the time you still have to go. If in the end I was sure that I would end up being your wife, that's how much you mean to me. I mean every word that I am saying; please believe me. As I said before, you can bring the subject up again, but please make sure that it is the right time and place.

It is just as hard for me to wait until I am married before I begin to have sexual relations, but I have learned that it is better to wait than to take chances. Let's forget that this ever happened and start acting and thinking like we have in the past.

Hope that I will receive a letter from you soon. I am still looking forward and planning for the day when I will become Mrs. Elijah Porter. This sounds wonderful.

Love and kisses to the sweetest man I know,
Margaret

March 9, 1953

Dearest Darling,

When you receive this letter, I hope it will make you as happy and cheerful as yours made me. It was a pleasure to hear from you after feeling so down and out for a couple of days. You had me worrying my head off, but after reading your letter, I felt better but still not as I did before.

No, I am not angry at you or anything like that. You had a reason for thinking the way you did and writing like that. It is all over and in the past, so let's forget about it. Only, I'll try not to get you that angry at me again. I just will have to watch myself very carefully. You always did mean what you say, so I understand, and I too am sorry for saying something like that in a letter. It should have never been said. Maybe if I had been near you, it would have been worse. But a letter is no place to talk like that. I didn't mean any harm, only being a little fresh at the wrong time.

I had not heard the news that made you so upset, and I only made matters worse for you.

My ink is running out, and I am getting sleepy. I'll finish tomorrow.

Be sweet.

Yours,
Porter

March 10, 1953

Dearest Darling,

After having a very bad week and hearing from you now makes me feel great. It wasn't a nice feeling; but now since your last letter, I have cheered up a bit. Since we have been together, I have never pressured you to do anything that you didn't want to do because then it would not be any fun for me. I like being with you and doing nice things. You know I love you by now. I keep telling you I do even if I sound as I don't sometimes. Loving you is all I can do when I am away for long times. It is hard, I know, to believe me, but I still tell you anyway that I do much more than you will ever know. Each day and night, I just keep hoping that someday, we can be together for keeps. Then this loneliness we share now won't seem so bad. Just a little more time and we will able to do all the things we wanted to do and couldn't.

I heard from Sherman a few weeks ago, and he was getting along OK. I know I won't be able to see him when he comes home for Easter, but tell him if you see him to have a wonderful time. I sure wish that I could be there with him.

This is all for now. I will write more next time.

Yours,
Elijah Porter

March 12, 1953

Dearest,

I received your letter today and was very glad to hear from you. You may not get this one until next week because mail won't leave until then. So far, since we have been out, we have had very nice weather. Only a few rainstorms, that's all.

You did make me suffer too; only it was my fault. I should have never asked you in a letter, but that is the way I am when I want to know something, I ask. That is the only way of learning something. I am sorry if I upset you by asking you in a letter. It was just a way in which I do things even if I hurt people. I don't mean to. I sure wouldn't have taken you up on what you said. I had too much to lose and nothing to gain by losing you. It didn't make me feel any good by reading a letter like that. It really made me feel sick inside. But now it is over, and we still have each other; that is all that matters for now.

This didn't make me prove that I love you. I do without this even coming up. I have a long time. Maybe not at first, but after seeing you and being with you, I have learned to care for you and love you as I want to be loved. Now I am sure it was right for me to have you that way. If I didn't, who knows what would have happened to me.

To get things right again is wonderful. We are going to keep forgiving each other for a whole month. I am sorry; you are sorry. I forgive you, and you forgave me. Now everybody is happy. Let's leave it that way. No more arguments in letters. The mailman gets a hard enough time without being shot at (smile). Mrs. Elijah Porter sounds nice; only it sounds nicer when you say it than it does when I say it.

Time is running short now. In a little while, lights will go out, so be sweet and keep smiling.

I love you as always.

Yours,
Elijah Porter

April 2, 1953

Dearest Elijah,

I received both of your letters yesterday, and they found me in the best of health, I hope when you receive this letter, you will be the same.

I am very glad that it made you happy to hear from me because I feel the same way when I hear from you. You will be surprised if you really knew how much I wanted to hear from you when I received them. They made me feel very good. Don't get yourself worried. I wasn't sick but I felt as though I needed to read a letter from you or even talk to you if I could.

How many times must I tell you that we aren't going to have any children right away, not even a year later. I want first of all for us to get married, then furnish off an apartment with good furniture. Then when that is all paid for, we can buy a house of our own. When the bills get low, only then we can have a family. you can't have a family and buy a house right away at the same time because children are very expensive. Do you want a home of your own or a house full of children first?

You said that the wedding is going be July 1955. Are you sure that you want it to be so soon after you get out of service? I didn't say that I really approved of the name baby. I just wanted you to feel good for a little while (smile).

Sherman came home yesterday, and he has about 25 days leave. Why can't you get that many days leave? He called me up this morning and talked to me for a long time.

Closing now with love, love, love, love, love, love.

Your darling Margaret, or Baby, whichever one.

Happy Easter, Darling, and here's hoping that you live to see many more. I hope with me though.

Margaret

May 12, 1953

Dearest Darling,

It's been a long time since the last time you heard from me, only a few days but still kind of long at that. We had a few baseball games last week. Mostly all of them were at night, so I couldn't get a chance to do much writing because I like to write at night better than daytime. Thinking is easier and mean more when I do write (smile).

Well, now that I haven't been home in a week, I want to come back again. I never do get tired of looking at you, never have and never will. I only see you a few days out of a year, and they go too fast. That is why I hate coming back here. But once I get back, I am OK. It is just that I never know when I will see you again. I just love you so much that whenever I am with you makes me feel that way. I like being with you all the time. When I am, I am completely happy until it is time to go. Then everything seems like the end. It is not the end for us. I know, but it seems like everything stops right there.

Margaret, I don't know how to put this into words, but I love you. I've loved you from the first time I kissed you, not as much as now. I know that I never felt this way about anybody in my whole life. I want you for my wife and for my children's mother. There isn't any other person I would want more than I want you. Maybe you will be happy with me. And maybe some things will make you feel different. Whatever comes, I want to share your troubles with you and kind of make them a little less important than they were. You mean all that and much more, which I can't put into beautiful words. The only words that I can put them in, which would be understandable, are "I love, Margaret. I love you. I love you with all my heart." If that isn't plain enough, I can't say it any plainer for you.

So, Baby, be a sweet little girl for me until I come home for always; and until June, we will have a wonderful time together.

I love you.

Yours,
Elijah Porter

May 25, 1953

Dearest Darling,

I received quite a few letters from you, but I have failed to answer them. Please forgive me, but you know how slow I am in answering letters. How have you been getting along? Fine, I hope. I have been doing as well as expected, I suppose.

How is the weather there? It is hot one day and cold the next. You really don't know what type of clothes to wear.

Everybody in your family is OK. But did you know that your grandfather died and that your father went to the funeral?

My cousin Irving is home until the 16th of July. Maybe you can get a chance to see him before he leaves. Are you sure that you will be home for the 4th July? As I want to go on my cousin's bus ride to Atlantic City, and I want you to go to. I had better start saving my pennies to buy a bathing suit because I don't have one. So you had better bring your swimming trunks with you when you come home.

I have started going to Church on weekdays again. I am going on Monday nights for five weeks, taking a course on Introduction to Teaching, which I am enjoying very much.

Well, I will close with my pen but not with my heart.

Love you as always,
Margaret

May 30, 1953

Dearest Darling,

When you didn't write me for a long time, I started to worry a little. Then I remembered that you said you are kind of lazy when it comes to letter writing. After that, it was OK.

There isn't anything new with me yet, the same old things going on. The only thing that gets me is two years. When it comes to being sure of things, I am. If I get home for the 4th of July, I'll be happy. I can't tell you that I will. My leave hasn't come thru. If it does, I may be with you then, but don't get all your hopes built up on it. I wouldn't want to disappoint you. You have been sweet, and I wouldn't want to spoil everything. I have never been to Atlantic City on a bus ride. People say it is a lovely place. Well, anyway, we will try to find out. One thing I want to see, I want to see if you look good in a bathing suit as you do in a dress (smile). This may be the only time that I'll get to see you, so I will try to come home then.

What are you going to teach when you finish school? I'll be your prize pupil, Francis and I.

I don't have much time to write today. I am on duty. I will write more next time.

Be sweet for I love you, Margaret.

Yours,
Elijah Porter

June 24, 1953

Dearest Darling,

Sometimes you put me on the spot. I don't mind answering your questions, but they may not come out right when I do answer them. I am no different than other fellows; only I know what I want when I get out.

The reason I don't talk to you about the future is because I am not sure myself. I mean if I make a lot of promises to you and don't keep them, you will be very angry, and I don't want to make any that I can't keep to you. But if you want to know, I'll give it to you straight; only don't take it as a promise. I don't want to build your hopes up. This is what I want to do when I get out.

First, I would like to get a place to live, furnish it, and get a good job. One in some business or a factory would do. I prefer business though. I will take whichever have the most advantages to me. After this, I want to get married to you of course. It won't take me but about two or three weeks to find some place to live, and if I don't, I still will have enough money to live on. I'll have six hundred dollars in cash when I get out, plus what I have saved up. That is well taken cared of so you don't have to worry about the money part.

I want to get married soon after I get out. I have waited too long now. We can plan out wedding and honeymoon plans so that we can have what you want. You wanted it straight, and here it is. Of course then, there will be a lot of love making and all that stuff after the wedding (smile).

The reason I want you and myself to do all what we want together is because that way, we both will know what the other want. So if something is not suitable to the other, we can get together on it. I would like for you to handle all of the money. You like that, don't you (smile)? I hate to say this but it is true. I am too easy, as you know that for yourself. If someone wants something from me, they keep asking and get it, like money or things, not someone I love. I don't give up that easy. I don't think I could give you up now or ever.

You wanted to know what the future holds for me; now you know. Like I said before, this is what I want to do. But something may happen, so it won't come out just as planned. If nothing happens, this is it, not a promise or nothing like that. I just want what I want, and that is you first and all the other stuff next. You will always come first to me. Without you, the other things don't mean anything to me.

Now that I have found someone who will be my wife and share my life, I want to marry her and try to make her happy. This is all I ask out of life. Love, happiness, and security.

This is what I want. If you see how we can change them, go ahead and speak. I am open for all suggestions. Let's both make the best of things that will befit both of us. That way, I know you will be happy; and when you are happy, I will be also. Remember, whatever I have is yours. all you have to do is ask for it. I love you that much, and if you still don't believe me, wait until the next time you see me and I will convince you.

So long for now and take care of yourself for me. Give your family my regards.

Be sweet, Baby.

Elijah Porter

June 24, 1953

Dearest Darling,

Getting your last two letters was kind of hard for me. The mail clerk didn't know if I was here. He had sent your letters back to the fleet office. It was getting so bad that I asked him if I were aboard. They have two Porters on ship, only one Elijah. Well anyway, we got that little matter straightened out fast.

I was coming home soon on leave, but you said it would be better to wait because you are going on your vacation. So I'll wait until you come back. This is for sure. I'll be up for the 4th of July. I want to see you anyway before you go away. I remember the last time you went away, and this time, I just feel like I want to see you real bad. I understand why you want to get away for a change of atmosphere.

You talk about your cousin; I would like to meet her. If she is as nice as you, she must be terrific (smile) because you are everything every guy should have. What am I talking about? "Every guy," that was wrong. What I mean is every Elijah Porter should have.

When I come home, I'll get to Newark about 2300 or 2400 Friday night. If it is before 2400, do you want me to call you? If not, I can wait until Saturday. There is a fellow here that has a car that lives in Newark, so we will drive up there in about 4 or 5 hours, all according to what time we catch the ferry.

Anyway, I'll get there if I have to fly by jet. There are other ways too (smile).

If you want to give a girl a present that means a lot to you, what would you give her for a going-away present? Now I don't want anything. What do you want for going away? An airplane, a jet, the moon or do you want some Chinese chop suey? Just name it, and I'll see what we have for a sweet girl. So you see, if I have you, I don't want anything else. All I want is to make you happy, and all I ask for is for you to be mine.

So long, Baby, and be sweet as you have always been. I still love you as much as ever and want you as much as ever, and want you in my crazy little way (smile).

You are still my little Baby, are you or are you not?

Yours always,
Elijah Porter

July 6, 1953

Dearest Darling,

If I never enjoy another 4th of July, I will always say I enjoyed this last one. It was what you would call a perfect day because you made it that way.

You know I didn't mind so much coming back this time. Maybe because you kept my mind off it by trying not to get angry at me (smile). I got down here in Norfolk in plenty of time, and I wasn't late this time either. I guess everybody thought that I was not a polite guy, rushing off like I did. Tell them I am sorry, but you know how fast that train left Newark. If it would have stayed a little longer, I could have given you a big kiss, but I'll get it later. I could only kiss you on your jaw.

But getting back to you. That was a wonderful lunch you fixed, and I was going crazy until I kissed you on the beach. I saw you in a bathing suit for the first time. I liked what I saw. I thought you would at least get your hips wet, but you wouldn't even get your feet wet. I don't know what I am going to do with you. Maybe it will be better if I married you then maybe you would trust me more to teach you how to swim. I wouldn't let anything happen to you. Honest, I wouldn't. I love you too much; you didn't seem to realize that. Well, if you are frightened of water, I am sorry. But I just wanted you to be happy, and if you can't swim, you just can't.

Next time when I come home, I won't wait until the last hour to start talking to you about something important and then have to leave.

Margaret, I am sorry but I can't write any more I am tired and sleepy tonight. I haven't slept since Thursday, so I'll turn in my rack now.

Tell my mother and father hello, and say that I wasn't looking sick either when I left. She will like that.

I love you always.

Elijah Porter

July 8, 1953

Dearest Darling,

In a few days, you will be going on your vacation. There is only one thing I am asking you is to have a good time and enjoy yourself, and when you come back, I'll be waiting for you. When you do get back, you can call me anytime. I'll be home no matter how late it may seem. That's if you want to call; if not, that is OK too.

You wonder sometimes why I say the things I do, like when I say I will always love you, and there will never be any other girl for me. Well, that is true. I only think of you as happy and lovable, not things that hurt. I don't want to think of them if something did happen to you. It would hurt me a whole lot. But like you said, I would get over it, but when is another story. I love you, Margaret, and if you dislike the way in which I do, then I am sorry. This the only true way in which I can love.

I know what I am doing because it is time for me to love you as deeply as I do even when I make you upset. I get a funny feeling like you are the reason why I want to do certain things and to be with you. It hurts to be here and still would like to be near you, but we can't do nothing about it now. Later on, we can see this time as being realist, and then we will know this was worth all the trouble and all the heartaches we both have gone through. I know it is hard on you because you are a girl, and I have too many other things to do. And thinking about that, it don't bother me all the time. Only when I relax I start thinking and wondering. Then I wonder about you. When you are sick, I am sick; and when you hurt, I hurt also. Everything that happens to you has an effect on me.

I am glad that I fell in love with you instead of someone else, as it could have been; but I am happy it was you, and I will always try to make you happy and protect you from all the rest of the wolves (smile).

So be my little girl and be sweet as you have always been.

Yours,
Elijah Porter

July 23, 1953

Dearest Darling,

When I couldn't come home last week, it made me very unhappy. There wasn't anything I could do but get upset and think up foolish ideas. That is why I called your mother as she and I are really good buddies (smile). I told her to put in a good word for me for I knew you would be disappointed when you came home. This way, you would at least know what is going on like you say you are very understandable at times when it comes to things we both can't help. Now I am waiting for the day when we can forget about this and make some of this come true right now. I am afraid to promise you anything or to say anything that I can't make come true. My time and life isn't my own. I don't want to make promises if I can't keep them. This is why I don't say anything to you or tell you a lot of news. I may build your hopes up and let you down. All I say and promise you this, I will always love you with the deepest devotion no matter how afar or how long we are apart.

I have lived to love you, and now that I need you, it makes this waiting worthwhile because when it is over, I'll know someone is waiting and wanting me as much as I want her. With this in mind, I can take the other two years happy (a little) and come out to a sweet little girl who is sweet and is worth having forever and forever. As long as I want you and you want me, I know that it can last forever and ever. But isn't it better to think that it can last forever and to look forward to that moment? At least if it doesn't, I can say I have loved and been loved; and now I am glad that a person I loved so much and wanted so badly was you, the kindest, most adorable girl I want because she is Margaret Williams, my little Baby.

Yours,
Elijah Porter

P.S. I love you.

August 3, 1953

Dearest Elijah,

I told you that I would write you a letter today, and I am sticking to my promise which I always do (smile). I was very much surprised to see you and also glad. You never know how much it means to me when you come home even if only for a short time.

On the weekend, it is very lonely, and I do get tired of sleeping all the time, believe it or not.

Only one thing that bothers me is when you have to leave, you are so impossible that I can't even stand to be around you because you make me angry every time I look at you. You have been in for two years and will be in for another two years, so why don't you give up the way you always look when you have to leave and be more pleasant than you are, and everything will be alright.

One thing that pleased me very much is that you asked my opinion before making any definite decisions, because in order for both of us to be happy, we will have to consult each other like that.

I want when you get out for us to furnish off an apartment with nice furniture, not some old cheap furniture, so that when we buy our house, we can still use the furniture; and it won't be falling apart. All we would have to do is add little extra odds and ends to make it look nice.

I forgot to tell you that I had a wonderful time in Coney Island, Saturday night, but we can go anywhere together for me to have a good time with you? I always do whenever I am with you except when you have to go back (smile).

I had better close now and get some work done. I was in bed by 9:30 PM after we left you at the station. Did you make good time getting back?

Yours as ever,
Margaret

August 7, 1953

Dearest Darling,

I received your letter yesterday, and it found me in the best of health just as you had hoped.

If feeling blue makes anything seem easier when you have to leave, then you better continue to feel that way; but if I had to feel like that, I don't think I would want to come home too often.

What I said Saturday night is true. When a fellow has used a girl in every possible way that he can, then he doesn't want her anymore; and when he gets ready to pick out a wife, 9 times out of 10 the one that he knows all about from head to toe won't be his wife because he will think that if she give him everything, then she would do the same with every other fellow.

I am determined more and more to keep myself as I have in the past because every marriage you hear of now, the girl is 4 to 6 months pregnant before she get married, and I don't want that kind of marriage. And the only way to be sure that I don't have that kind is not to do the things in which you can become that way. I am sorry if I sound so hard on you, but that is the way things is and that is the way I want them to stay. I've told you what I want to do when we get married, and we can't do those things if we have a family before we ever really know what married life consist of. As long as you treat me like you have in the past, you don't ever have to worry about losing me.

Sherman came over to my house on Wednesday evening and visited with me for a while.

All of our tickets for the bus ride are out. Now we are waiting to get paid for them. Still wish you were here to go with us.

Yours as Ever,
Margaret

August 8, 1953

Dearest Darling,

By now, you are wondering why I haven't answered your letter. Well, when I was home, I thought I told you we would be out for a few weeks; so our mail wouldn't go off until we hit a mailing port.

You seem to always keep your promises when you make one, and I was very glad to hear from you. I know you would be surprised to see me; that's why I didn't let anyone know that I was coming home. If I did, I may not have made it, and that would have been terrible (smile). Waiting this long is enough without keep fooling you and building your hopes up. So when I come home, you will not know until I get there. That way, you will never have to expect me and plan something, and then you will be disappointed by me not showing up.

Margaret, I am sorry that you feel the way you do when I have to leave. You should not get angry with me. It is hard to leave you after I get to enjoy myself. Every time I leave, it seems like I am leaving for good instead of just a little while. I try not to show myself, but it comes out just the same. The last time, you had me a little worried. I thought I would have to leave without saying "so long" to you (smile).

Sherman told me you were coming over, but still I was very impatient. Everybody kept asking me questions and saying things, and I didn't feel like talking; they talk too much when I have to leave.

When I get out, I will have about two thousand five hundred dollars. That should be enough to get married and furnish an apartment with nice furniture, shouldn't it? This will be all the money I saved up while I was in service. I'll get a job and take care of both of us. So see, I do think about the future after being in here for four years. Work will seem easy (smile).

I enjoyed myself in Coney Island too. Only if it could have lasted a little longer, I would have liked it much more. I am glad you enjoyed yourself. When you do, I get awful happy inside. Just seeing you smile makes me a very happy guy.

So be sweet until I see you again, which I hope is soon. I still love you as much as ever and always will forever and ever.

Yours,
Elijah Porter

August 15, 1953

Dearest Darling,

Your letter found me very happy and glad to be back in Norfolk after being out for a week.

Feeling blue does makes everything seem easier. You see, if I didn't feel sad and unhappy, you would think something was the matter, like I didn't miss you like I say that I do. You wouldn't want to see me go away happy and glad to leave you now, would you? This is the way I show you that I do mean what I say. I miss you, and I do love you a whole lot.

By now I should know when you say something, you mean it. If you didn't, you wouldn't be you. I understand you want to get married the right way and nothing to force you. That way, you will be getting what you want. You have seen a few messed up marriages, and from the way you talk and act, you don't want one. I don't myself, and if I have anything to do with any of this, none of this will happen. I know that you want only the best of your married life. I can wait a little longer, and sometimes you are hard on me. And then again, you are easy. I shouldn't say that (smile). You may get a little rougher, but what can a hundred-and-ten-pound little girl do (smile)? One thing for sure, whenever you make up your mind, that is it. There is no way of changing it. I'll have to remember that in the future.

Sometimes, I do make you angry with me, but I hope I never make you angry enough for you to leave me. That would hurt too much. When I make you angry again, do me a favor. Hit me on the head with a rolling pin (smile). It won't hurt, but it will do a little good.

So Sherman finally went over to see you. Well, give him a ribbon. Give your family my regards and tell Catherine I'll send her some writing paper when I get paid next payday. I am a poor sailor.

Be sweet and take care of yourself. I love you.

Yours,
Elijah Porter

October 30, 1953

Your most adorable letter was received yesterday, and I am very glad to say that it found me in the best off health but a little lonesome without you. When you receive this letter, I hope that you will be fine also.

I am glad that you left early so that you could get back on time, and that we didn't have to worry whether the bus came on time or not as you still had plenty of time.

By the way, I did go back to the choir on Wednesday night, and they accepted me back as a member. On the way to church, I met Governor, and when I told him that I was going back after being out for a long time, he said that they should send me back home and say that I am too late for them to accept me again.

You know that you really get on my nerves sometimes. Suppose you didn't take that money that I gave to you, what would you have done to get something to eat? You know that is a long trip from here to Norfolk, and you do have to eat sometime, you know. Can I ever get into that wonderful head of yours that when I have some money and you need it, that you can have it and that you needn't be afraid to ask for it or to accept it when I offer it to you.

My mother even asks me when you leave, do you have enough money to get back, and did I offer you some money to make sure that you had enough, and if she thinks that I should give you some money in these circumstances, don't you think that you should take it?

Love you.

Your Darling,
Margaret

November 2, 1953

Dearest Darling,

Sitting here, rereading your letter, I got to thinking, I was going to wait until tomorrow to answer it. Tonight, we have a good movie, *Shane*. It has been on here, three times already, so I let him go tonight and answer your letters. This is more important than Shane.

For a while I was getting worried. You always wait until I write first, then you answer. That is OK, but I hope that I didn't upset you that much while I was home (smile).

I always leave from up there in plenty of time, so I can come back again. It does me a lot of good coming back on time too. Everybody is happy, and you are too.

So you finally went back to the choir at church again. If I was them, I wouldn't have taken you back. Who said that you could sing anyway (smile)? Now they are going to have a messy choir with you up there, but what a church they will have now, a little spit fire in the noisy part (smile).

If I hadn't taken that money, my big intestine would have eaten my little intestine from hunger. You can get into my head that I can have what you have, and all you have to do is keep trying. Maybe you will convince me. I never ask you for anything because I always could find some way out of something. Only this time, you caught me. I don't like to ask you for money. It isn't right. I know we are going to get married, but a fellow must have a little pride. I don't know what you call it. Maybe I am crazy, but that is the way I am. You have a wonderful mother. I like her as if she was my own, and I do understand it was hard to ask you the first time; and I am still living, so don't worry about it. Next time, I will ask you just for drill so you will be happy (smile).

Yours,
Elijah Porter

P.S. Don't mind the wise cracks. They are not to be thought about again, but I still say you can't sing (smile). Also, tell your Uncle Ralph hello.
8

---

[8] Elijah was right; I could not sing. Mount Calvary Baptist Church encouraged all their people to sing and to be part of church. Growing up in church helped me to stay a strong young woman.

November 8, 1953

Dearest Darling,

When you receive this letter, I hope it will find you in the best of everything. Things are not too bad down here. The weather is cold, and it rains most of the time. For a few days, I thought winter was still here. It came so sudden, and no one was expecting it. It is a good thing that we will be leaving soon.

Yesterday, we all had to put in chits for leave; and for the holidays, they wanted to know what time we wanted to leave like last year. I picked New Year's only. I won't be able to stay too long because we have a place to be right after New Year's. I should tell you the day I'll get up there, but now I'll keep you in suspense for a little while. But in a few weeks from now, I'll tell you or maybe not, then either. I think I'll just drop in like Santa Claus (smile).

I am glad that we will be away from Norfolk most of the winter. There is too much water around here, and it gets really cold during January and March. Where we are going is home again. You know Cuba and the islands around there? That is why I can't spend too much time home for New Year's. Thanksgiving and Christmas are long, and I could get a few more days, but if I took one of them, I couldn't be home for New Year's. So I'll try to spend those few days with you if anything comes up different so I can't come, then I'll let you know before you decide what your plans for us will be, and that way, you will not have to change anything from the plans that you have made.

Since I have known you, we have never spent a Christmas together. One day, we will. Now that day seem a long way off. When it does come, I hope it will be one well remembered.

So be my little girl and take care of yourself. I still love you and always.

Elijah Porter
9

---

9 We never spent Christmas together until December 25, 1955, after we were married. The first Christmas was in 1950 and that was the year that I was in Georgia, and Elijah wrote me my first love letter. Elijah was in the Navy for the next four Christmases and did not ask for it off as I always wanted him to spend New Year's with me.

Letters (1954)

January 28, 1954

Dearest Elijah,

I am trying to get in the habit of writing to you a little more than I have in the past since you claim that you receive very little mail.

When you receive this letter, I hope that you will be pleased in hearing from me as I am always pleased to hear from you.

My sister Catherine graduated from high school last night, and now she is out on her own.

I haven't done anything since you were home last. I keep asking people to go out with me, and they won't, so I got tired of asking and went to the movies alone. Elijah, I shouldn't tell you this, but I am so bored until I don't know what to do. It's the same old thing day in and day out. Go to work and back home. Go to church and back home. I love church, but I need to have some fun with people, which makes me miss you more.

Next weekend, Iona and I are planning on going out for my birthday. I hope that Josh will let her go with me as it would be nice to go out for my birthday. There is a dance at Wide A Way Hall, and I am thinking of going since I haven't been anywhere lately.

Can you imagine February 26th we will have been dating for four years and still have eighteen months to go before we can get married?

I am closing this letter now and hope to see you soon.

Love you forever,
Margaret

February 10, 1954

Dearest Darling,

Sometimes you worry your pretty little head too much, you know. I'll be alright but still you worry about me if I am in Norfolk or Cuba. Anyway, it is nice to know someone worry about me even if I am not worth it, or am I?.

The weather in Cuba is hot all the time. Sometimes it drops down to 70 degrees, then it is cold.

I had a nice time there. About ten of us went out together that way. It didn't cost too much. We rented a cab all day for ten dollars. We went all over the place, only the prices are something. They are just like those back in the states. It was a real nice trip there even if we stayed only a few days.

I sent that silverware off last week. By now, you should have received it, and I didn't forget it either. I would have sent it sooner but didn't have enough time to pick it up. I hope you like it because I do, and if you don't, then we will have to get something different. These will be OK for everyday for us to use; we can get some better ones for company.

I love you, Margaret, and I am glad I can do some of the things you ask me to do. Maybe that is the reason I do. You have never asked to do anything that seemed impossible or unlawful (smile). So you see, I love you not only for what you ask me to do but because you are my girl, and I what to make you happy. And that way, I could be happy to. I do not want ever for you to be unhappy. Then, I would feel that my world is coming to an end.

It won't be long now before we will be together for good and then you will be happy. I know it seems like a long time to wait, but after it is all over, you will never know it took you this long to hook me into marrying you (smile).

Until then, I hope you can wait just a little while longer. It won't be easy; I know. But anyway, I hope it will be a shorter wait and a long life together, that is, if you don't kick me out for bothering you all the time.

Well, honey, I will be closing for now. I'll see you soon, I hope.

Yours,
Elijah Porter

February 10, 1954

Dearest Darling,

Thank you very much for the lovely set of silverware; it is just what I wanted.

There is only one thing that is wrong, and that is I didn't receive any tablespoons with the set. I got 6 knives, 6 soup spoons, 6 forks, 6 salad forks, 1 large salad fork and 1 large salad spoon. I also got 6 teaspoons.

If there is any way that you can check to see if I should have gotten some other pieces, please do so; or tell me how to do it, and I will. Here is the numbers that were on the set.

S15448 B 2 Z23725
$27.00

If there wasn't supposed to be any, then I will have to try and get some that would match this set.

Love you,
Margaret

February 10, 1954

Dearest Darling,

You don't know how happy you make me feel when I write and you are OK. I feel wonderful knowing there isn't anything to worry about, but I still worry just like you (smile).

Don't feel bad because I said you were lazy for not writing more often. I understand and won't bother you anymore. I was just kidding you anyway, but it is nice to hear from you. Anytime you write me is OK, I won't be angry at you.

When you go to Utica, tell Ruth hello; maybe I'll get a chance to see her again before I get hitched (smile). She is real nice, only crazy about her soldiers (the bums). You asked me if I could be home for June 6th; well, that is kind of hard to say. It is too far for me to decide. If I can, I will let you know beforehand. Now I can't make any plans for sure. Every time I do, they back fire, so don't be disappointed if I can't make it.

So now my Baby is twenty years old. How does it feel (smile)? You are still my little girl. If you do get kind of old, you will always be because you can't gain any weight (smile). I don't mind. You are alright the way you are, plenty of room in my arms for you. I am just a little too fresh, huh? You don't know how fresh; maybe I can keep you in suspense until we get married. For now, I love kissing you all the time. Well, I can't help it if you make me love you so much I just can't help myself. So long for now and be sweet for me. I still feel the same about you. I just love you, Baby.

Yours always,
Elijah Porter

February 14, 1954

Dearest Darling,

After sleeping mostly all day, I thought that I would answer your letters. It was real nice to hear from you; they found me very happy, as you wished.

For a while there, I thought you didn't get the silverware, but I guess I was a little too impatient on getting it to you. I was glad that you liked it very much. I thought for sure that there were some table-spoons. I won't have time to check until Wednesday. I'll order some from the PX if they don't have any in stock. They had another set on display, but it costs a little too much for the few sets. We'll get some more some other time; these are for us to start off with.

There are a lot of small things that we can use. If you can think of any more, let me know. If they are not too large, then I can send it to you. If they are too large, then I can't. They only let certain things go out from here, and if I go into Norfolk, the prices are up in the sky; so I buy my stuff on the base. It is much cheaper and better.

Well, so long for now, honey. I'll be seeing you soon.

Yours always,
Elijah Porter

March 8, 1954

Dearest Darling,

When you receive this letter, I hope it will find you as happy as I am. I left so fast last night that I don't think I said goodbye. It was kind of sudden to leave like that. Anyway, we got back OK. We drove the speed limit all the way down here. We got on the ferry and caught a few winks of sleep, and I had enough money to get back on time. I didn't spend too much this time because we didn't go any-place. If you wanted to, I don't think I could have taken you as I was kind of broke. You understand that you will have a broke husband if you marry me (smile)? Better change your mind before it is too late; maybe later it will be too late.

There is no reason for me to tell you. I was glad to see you and be home. I am always glad to be with you even if it is only for a short time. That is why being away hurts so much, only a short time with you and back here again. It all seems like a dream, only it isn't because I know now it was no dream. I know you didn't want me to leave you, but after seeing you, I can take it easy. I just came on back and didn't worry about it. After all, I must come back anyway, so I better stop worrying, right?

I love you very much, and if I seem like I don't sometimes, I still do. I will always love you and feel like I do. If I didn't, I wouldn't enjoy myself when I am with you. So you see, I do love you, and this why I want to make you my little wife. Maybe I can make you happy. I'll try awful hard if you will give me a chance.

Be sweet for me and take care of yourself for me.

Yours,
Elijah Porter

March 14, 1954

Dearest Darling,

By the time you receive this letter, I will be on my way back down south. It will be a long trip but worth the trouble. When I get back, a few months will have past. They go by fast when we are out to sea, maybe that is why I like to travel. Sometimes, I shouldn't worry about how much time that I have to do, but each month makes my time shorter and shorter so that I am always looking forward to the time I can return to you for good. If I were not thinking of you all the time, maybe it wouldn't be so bad, but I do. And it is good because when I think of you, everything I do and think seem nice, and I don't feel so awful at times. That is the only way I have of remembering you, as I want to remember you.

When we get married, maybe then you will see why I want to get out of here. There is nothing wrong, but after looking at that last picture of you, I know this is no place for me because I have sweet little girl who loves me as much as I love her. Maybe you think I don't because I stay away most of the time. If you only knew how much I love and miss you, you would understand, No matter how long or how far I may go, I will always love you. Margaret, if I didn't, then I couldn't say these things. I love you so much that I feel lonesome even in a crowd. I know I will never be able to be with you all the time and tell you how I feel about you.

I hope you remember that it is you I love, and you are the one I want to marry. Not that I think it is right, but I love you and want too. I want to try and make you happy. In that way, I will be happy, and make all these days and nights we have spent away from each other worthwhile.

I hope that I can be the kind of husband that you want. If you want me, I am willing to try awful hard to live up to your idea of your kind of husband.

Be sweet and take care of yourself for me. I don't want anything to happen to you now or ever. If it did, all of this would seem like a bad dream.

Sincerely yours always,
Elijah Porter

March 26, 1954

Dearest Darling,

While sitting down thinking of the sweetest person I know and the one I love, I decided to drop him a few lines, which means this letter is for you.

I am fine and hope when you receive this letter that you will be the same. Today is quite a rainy day; how is the weather where you are?

I called your mother today, and she was fine and so was the rest of your family.

Elijah, I saw a beautiful bedroom suite that I would like to have. It is a bed with one headboard but has two separate beds which are close together. I know that you disapprove of twin beds but won't you please look at them anyway when we go to buy furniture and see if you like them or not. I would like to have them very much, but I wouldn't force you to have them if you really didn't want them because I want you to be happy also. I wouldn't pick anything out without you being with me to agree on buying it.

Have you heard from your brother Sherman because your mother said that she hadn't heard from him in quite a while?

I am leaving to go to Utica on the 16th of April and will be gone until the 20th of April. I hope I have as good a time as I have in the past. I think that it will be a long time before I go back again.

Love & kisses to you,
Margaret

March 27, 1954

Dearest Darling,

When you receive this letter, I hope it will find you in the very best of everything. It is rather hot down here. From your last letter, you said it was cold up there. Well, I haven't been in any cold weather for quite some time now. By the time we get back, it will be summer.

Margaret, you don't know how happy I was when I got your letters a few days ago. We were at a place called Roosevelt Roads, Puerto Rico, when they arrived. I wanted to answer them right then, but it was awful hot and I was kind of tired from Saturday watches. We only stayed there for a few days before coming back here to Virginia.

You asked me how many boys I could get to be in the wedding, well, as many as you need because all of them will be out of service before then.

When I come home, Christmas or New Year's, I'll bring enough money to buy most of the small items we will need for a start. I may get New Year's because it is kind of hard to get Christmas leave. It seems that they all want to be home for the 25th. Well, I'll be alright if I get New Year's day off. It doesn't make much difference to me which one I get.

So far, I haven't been to a place where they still have those bags. If we do, I'll get you one. The places we were at were Naval Operation Bases for the Atlantic Fleet. Maybe next week, we will get some good liberty.

So long for now

Yours,
Elijah Porter

March 30, 1954

Dearest Darling,

Your last letter found me very happy, and I hope this one will find you the same. I must admit you said some nice things about me, better watch out (smile).

From the way you sound, you make me think bad things. I like twin beds, the ones with one headboard but not the ones with a table in the middle like the ones you and Catherine have. I'll be home in July and look at them, but if you like them the way you say you do, it will be OK by me. As I said before, it will be your house as much as mine, but this is the women's department. It doesn't have much to do with men. We both like mostly the same things, so it won't be too hard to get something that we both like.

I haven't heard from Sherman in a long time myself; we don't get each other's mail until about a month after it has been mailed.

By the way, what made you think you won't be going back to Utica after this for a long time? Just because you get married doesn't mean you have to give up all of your trips. Go ahead and leave your husband; maybe he will love your cooking better after he eat his for a few days and save those kisses for later. I'll collect COD.

I had something I wanted to tell you that happened to me down here. I was going to wait until I came home. If I started it and didn't finish, you would get angry. We were out Roosevelt Roads last week when the Base Police came to the ship to get me about a phone call from the States. I thought that someone in my family or yours was sick from the way they were talking. Then when we got over there, they explained it to me.

Someone either on there or on the base made a phone call back to the States and didn't pay for it. They used my name, so they thought it was me. But I think I convinced them it wasn't because I hadn't been off the ship that day. Now I don't care because we left a few hours later; they really had me worried there for a while. On my way over there, a million thoughts were going on in my mind. I didn't know what to think. Well anyway, it is all over. But you were likely to lose your Elijah to the Puerto police. So you better hold on to me real tight (smile). One of the offices here told me to forget it and don't worry about it. I did stop worrying but have not forgotten it. I sure want to leave here now. This place is too hot in many more ways than some others. Oh, the bill for the phone call was for fifty-some dollars. That is why they wanted the guy that made the call, only not this Elijah Porter.

Be sweet and keep loving me. Will you, Baby?

Elijah Porter

April 1, 1954

Dearest Elijah,

I received five letters from you last Saturday, and I must say that I was very happy to receive every one of them. They found me in the very best of health, and I sincerely hope that mine will find you the same.

You think that I begin to worry when I do not hear from you, but I really don't anymore especially when you tell me that you won't be able to send any mail out. Because I know that when I do receive, some of it will be a lot at one time.

As far as thinking that you have stopped loving me, that is not true because we both love each other so much to stop now.

In one of your letters, you had asked me when do I think that the wedding will take place. It's four to six weeks after you have been discharged, which would be the last week in July or the second week in August. Do you think that this will give you enough time to buy your clothes and do the other things that you want to do?

If things go the way that I am hoping and praying that they will. This is what I think that we will be able to do. I figure that we will have enough money to pay cash for all of our furniture except a television. My mother said that they would give us the television. If we can do this, then we can buy a car right away. I think that we should buy one especially since you will be going to school, then you won't have to stand and wait for the buses. You can drive the car to get home to your darling wife that much faster (smile). What do you think of these ideas?

The money that we would be paying on the furniture each month can go toward a car. Please write me right back, or as soon as possible, and let me know what you think of these things. Tell me because you might have a better suggestion than I do. None of these things have to be as I have stated them, but you work harder and much better when you know exactly what you are working for.

With love,
Margaret

April 6, 1954

Dearest Darling,

After being down here in this place for this long, I am ready to leave. It wouldn't be so bad if we didn't have to play so much war. That's what keeps me up all hours at night; it really gets you. But it won't be like this for long. In a few more days, we will be leaving this place.

You answered all of my questions and cleared up a few things for me. If we get married when you said we would, that will give me enough time to buy my clothing and get the other things; it won't take me long.

If we do have enough money to pay cash for furniture, I think we should wait until the first of the year to get a car, or maybe you like the 1955-model car. Anyway will be alright with me. The other ideas are OK too. Now all we have to do is hope that everything else come out alright, and as you said, I can get home to my darling wife that much faster. But she may be sleeping when I get there, so it won't do much good, will it (smile)? Only if you don't mind being awaken for something (smile).

Before I come home for Christmas, I'll draw enough money so we can buy most of the small items. Then you won't have to worry about them later. I still will have enough money left to do other things, and I won't have to bother any of my other money. Now all I have to is to get out and come back to you.

Love you,
Elijah Porter

April 16, 1954

Dearest Darling,

When you receive this letter, I hope you will be happy and back home safe. You said you were going to Utica for Easter, and I do hope you had a wonderful time.

So far, we have been traveling around here, and no place to go. Everywhere you look, there is nothing but water. Maybe by next week, we should be in Moorehead.

Here is the money that you asked me for. I wanted to send it off before now, but I couldn't. Maybe you will get it before the 22nd. I am sending it in cash because you may need it before you can get to the bank; then again, all of the banks or stores may be closed so I hope you do get it before then. If we don't pull into a port soon, I know that you won't. But I am hoping that we do.

How much money did Uncle Sammy take from you this time? He took one hundred and twenty eight dollars from me, and I got back six dollars and fifty cents. He could have kept that as it doesn't do me any good (smile).

Well so long, Margaret, and be sweet; and I'll be seeing you soon, I hope.

Always yours,
Elijah Porter

April 18, 1954

Dearest Darling,

Today was Easter Sunday, and I hope yours was better than mine. We are still moving around out here, going someplace. Maybe we will get there, and maybe not. I know there hasn't been any mail leaving here since we left Viaques, so if you don't get any, don't worry about it. I'll let you know when we are back in Norfolk.

You know something, I missed you more this past six weeks than I did when we were over in the Med. I don't know why, but every time I go to sleep, I had a lot of crazy dreams. Some of them were awful. I sure wanted to see you but couldn't. I guess that is because I am always thinking of what I would like to do when I get out. Whatever it is, I missed you a lot.

I love you and want to marry you. If that what's make me want to get out of here in a hurry, then I am happy just to know that I have someone waiting for me. It makes me feel good when things seem to go wrong. Maybe you don't know it, but you have a lot to do with the way I feel and think. I feel like I want to hold you forever and kiss you, but I know I can't. It is nice just thinking of it anyway. Margaret, I just want to be with you and just talk about anything I'll be happy then. But I can't, and when I want you the most, I can't have you. That's what makes me worry so much and want to get out of here. Don't get me wrong now. I like this outfit, but every time I look at your picture, or read one of your letters, I know this is no place for me.

Well anyway, I'll try to take this until next June, then someone else can have it. Be sweet for me, Margaret, and remember, honey, I will always love you.

Give everybody my regards.

Always yours,
Elijah Porter

April 23, 1954

Dearest Elijah,

I received your letters and was very glad to hear from you. I am fine.

Thank you ever so much for the money. I was beginning to worry about what I was going to do. It is going to be two days late, but as long as they get it before 31 days, it is alright. I hope that I didn't put you to too much trouble.

How was Easter with you? Did you have a good time? My Easter was really enjoyable, as you know I went to Utica, and everyone showed me a wonderful time.

In one of your letters, you mentioned that I must really have some nice furniture in mind or that I have been looking at. To be truthful, I haven't really looked for any. The things that I mentioned to you, I just happened to see them while shopping for something else.

As for my income tax, I paid four hundred and some dollars. Of which, I got back $35.12 which I deposited into the bank.

I am at work, but I had to write you right back to let you know that I received the money.

Thanks again.

Loving you always,
Margaret

May 4, 1954

Dearest Darling,

That letter you were talking about got here yesterday afternoon. I wasn't expecting it so soon. Anyway, it was nice to hear from you.

I am sorry you got the wrong idea last Sunday. I do want to come home for Christmas or New Year's but from the way I was talking and acting, you didn't think so. One of these holidays, I'll be home so we can get out like you said and get some of the little things out of the way. I'll try to get about ten or fifteen days for when I do come home.

Margaret, since my mind is a little clearer. I thought this would be a good idea. Let me know how you like it. I'll be home in July, so why not check and find out about the hall and about how much it will cost. I mean, we don't have to put a deposit down unless they want one. We can find out which place will be best, and I can also get a few ideas about the honeymoon. Then you will not have so much to do. I know it is kind of early to do all of these things, but if you want to do them in July, or December, it's OK by me. But I thought since I'll be home soon and have a long leave, it will be better to do them. Then we can also find out how much money we will have left. I mean, a better idea then we had before because after you showed me how much we will have left, I was a little afraid; and Margaret, I do want to take you on a honeymoon even if we have to give up something else.

I know it is only one day, but I want you to remember it. It will be worth all of this, and I think you do deserve a rest because if I know you, you will be dead tired when it is all over. Even if we can only stay a few days, it will be OK by me as long as we take a trip together.

I am still not sure of the people to be invited to the wedding. Things happen so fast on Sunday I forgot a little. I'll make a list out and let you check it with yours because I am sure I left off some real close friends. I didn't know you had all that figured out until I came home. That shows how much I don't know about you. There is still a lot more I can find out about you if I could only stay around you a little more often.

Don't be too hard on me. I've never been around weddings and all those things, but since I am getting married soon, I see there is a lot I have to learn, and you have to teach me. I learn fast if you have the patience to teach a hard head like me.

Margaret, I am getting tired, and I have the duty today. I'll write some more tomorrow.

Yours now and always,
Elijah Porter

May 9, 1954

Dearest Darling,

When you receive this letter, I hope you will be happy and as lovely as ever. By now, you are in church or on your way there. That is where I should be because I haven't gone since Easter Sunday. We had a small service in here but that was the first I attended in a long time. Isn't that terrible?

This Sunday sure is different. For some reason, it seems not like the last weeks at all. Maybe I need to go over the hill and come to see you (smile). OK, I'll be up there in a few hours (smile). That's if I can catch a fast seagull going north.

Margaret, you remember telling me about buying a car? Well, I was thinking the other day. We won't have enough money left over to buy one, so why not let it go until we can save a little more money and get settled down? That way, we won't be in a hole in case something else comes up which we didn't expect to happen. I can manage going to school without one for a while, and I won't be away from you too long because you will be asleep anyway when I come home.

For a little girl, you sure can make a person love you in a big way. Ever since I came back, you are all I have been thinking about. If I try to sleep, you always enter my mind, smiling and teasing me all the time. Maybe that is the way you have of punishing me for being bad to you, teasing me. You know how badly I want to be with you and can't. Boy, what a life. Anyway, you better enjoy it now because later on, you will be tired of me all the time. Then what will you do? Kill me or give to the junk man?

So long for now, honey. I'll be seeing you in a few more months. Don't be expecting me either. I want to surprise you in July (smile).

Yours always,
Elijah Porter

May 14, 1954

Dearest Elijah,

When you receive this letter, I hope that you will be as well as I am.

How is the weather today? Here, it is quite cloudy and looks like rain. We haven't been having too much nice weather. It is very dark and dreary.

We are planning on having a party on the 25th of June, which will make three years of service life for you and three years of loneliness for me. But after one more year, everything will be fine, I hope. After all this time, we should make the perfect couple. Don't you think so?

I saw the kind of kitchen set that I would like, and I also saw a table for the living room. I can hardly wait until I am busy buying and fixing up an apartment for us; something that we can call ours.

Ralph and his friend are giving a party in our basement on May 28th. My father is fixing up the basement for them, and it is going to look nice.

Closing now with all my love.

Margaret

May 23, 1954

Dearest Darling,

Yesterday, I received three letters from you. We had been out for a few days on a trial run. Now we are back in Little Creek for a while.

You said that you are having a party on the 25th of June. I hope you won't be celebrating my three years away because I don't see how I did it after looking back at it. I don't want to go through that again; one more year seem long enough.

If we don't make the perfect couple, you can always trade your husband in for a new one (smile), but he may not love you as much as this one does. He stays away most of the time, but when he does come home, he tries to make up for lost time. Then before you know, it is time to depart; that makes things much more difficult.

It seems like I won't see you again, so you start getting lonely and I get restless, but don't worry too much I know you are getting impatient, but try to take it for a little longer.

Well, this is about all from a lonely guy. Now I better close before you have to pay an extra six cents (smile).

Be sweet for me, honey.

Yours,
Elijah Porter

June 7, 1954

Dearest Darling,

When you receive this letter, I hope you will be rested up a little. Of course you were glad to get rid of me so you could get some rest (smile).

For a while there, Sunday, I had you kind of worried about me getting back on time. We made it back OK, and on time, so you can stop worrying and wondering if I made it on time. It was kind of late to be leaving Newark even with three hours to spare. Next time, I will get a sure ride. Then, you will not have to wait and get impatient with me. Every time I get down there with you, I can't talk for some reason or another.

Margaret, you don't know how happy you made me this weekend. I was so overjoyed with the furniture you showed me that I couldn't sleep the whole time that I was there. I think it is real nice, and it isn't too high either. The way you talked about it, I thought it was just another outfit. Then when I saw it, you could have knocked me over with a feather. That is how surprised I was. That wasn't all that made me so happy. The way you talked to me and explained things were nice. I am a lucky guy to have such an understandable girl as you. It makes me feel awful good when I am with you, and you are not angry at me. This weekend was well-spent, and I truly hope you enjoyed it as much as I did.

Give my regards to everyone and be sweet, honey. I still love you as much as always even if you are expensive (smile).

Yours,
Elijah Porter

P.S.
One year, 18 days, 8 hours and 30 minutes, and I'll be yours for always unless you think different (smile).

June 20, 1954

Dearest Darling,

When you receive this letter, I hope it will find you well and not to tired. We came back to Little Creek late Friday night.

I hope that you got the money alright. We left in a hurry, and I thought it wouldn't get off before we came back, and I wanted to get it to you as fast as I could.

Last night, I went over to Norfolk to have dinner with Bibb and his wife. They asked me if I would because Mrs. Bibb had heard so much about Porter that she wanted to meet me.

A few of the other fellows are here, and we went fishing down by the NOB. It was about night when we came back, and guess what, I drove most of the way back. As it is country and the roads are clear, Bibb let me drive. I didn't have a driving license, so he took over after we got back into the city. Next week, I am going over to Portsmouth and take a driver's test. That's if I have the three dollars. Between all of us last night, we only had four dollars, and that went for gas.

I had a nice time, as the last time I was in Norfolk for liberty was two years ago. I don't care much for the place; it is too much like Broome Street.

Just think ten more days, and I'll be home again. It seems far away, but I will be glad to see you again. This time, we won't have to rush things too fast. It has been almost a year since I had leave last; that is because this year is going real fast.

Margaret, you said that your mother and father were going away on the 2nd of July. Do you think you can be alright while they are away? If I am able to be there, then I will take care of you and be a good guy (smile).

Tell everybody hello and to stop eating so much hard candy. I still love you even if you have another boyfriend that you are going to marry. If you love him as much as you do me, then that is OK. I'll beat his head in (smile).

So long, honey.

Yours,
Elijah Porter

July 19, 1954

Dearest Darling,

I know that you will be surprised to hear from me so soon, but I couldn't resist the opportunity of writing this letter.

Your visit was enjoyed very much, only I will be very happy when all these visits and goodbyes are over.

Elijah, I hope that you are happy and pleased about the kind of reception I planned to have because it is something, that I have always wanted when I get married.

I also want you to know that I appreciate you trying to help me in everything that I attempt to do. I hope that you don't think I am going too fast, but I want us to have accomplished something in the four years of our waiting before marriage.

If we have the bedroom suite and the pots & dishes paid for before we get married, we will have accomplished quite a bit.

When two people want something, they have to work together. One can't want one thing, and another wants something different. In that way, you'll never gain anything really because you don't know what you both want. Thank you very much for everything you did for me; you'll never know how much it means to me.

By the way, what time did your bus come? I am sorry that I had to leave, but remember if I don't work, we won't have as much as we want.

Your loving wife-to-be to my ever loving husband-to-be,
Margaret

July 20, 1954

Dearest Darling,

When you receive this letter, I hope it will find you as happy as you were yesterday, and all the other days.

You were looking kind of sad when we parted, but you shouldn't have. I didn't want to leave. I got back here about seven o'clock last night, so I had time to get all of my gear squared away. We made very poor time getting back; the bus stopped too much for me.

Anyway, it is all over for a while, and we must start to living dreams instead of reality. It was nice, and I enjoyed my short visit with you very much. You made me very happy, and I love you for it. I couldn't take you out much, but you understood why I couldn't. It was still nice just being with you. By now, you must be tired of me saying I love you all the time. If you are, then I am sorry. I can't help it for I do love you so much, and being with you for such a short time that I have to say it over and over. That way, you will feel like I love you because they are not only words. Words don't mean anything if you don't have a strong feeling for them.

I am sorry that I couldn't take you out Sunday to get some Chinese food. I should have told you that I didn't have much money. By now, I should know you would understand, but I didn't tell you so you were a little disappointed. I didn't want to buy it for you anyway. I asked you for three years to eat some Chinese food with me and you wouldn't. I went away and you ate some food with someone else (smile). I am not angry, and you shouldn't be. Next time I am home, I'll get some for you. OK, sweetheart?

Did your boss say anything to you for coming in late to work on Monday? I hope he didn't because you went to the station with me. You won't listen to me. I try to tell you not to come with me but you always do, and you know something, I like for you to come with me (smile). I just keep saying don't and hope you say no so that I can ask you. Smart, huh?

When we were in the movie, Sunday, I was thinking awful hard then that I was on a bus leaving that night for Norfolk; and I wanted to talk. After that, I know I couldn't leave without seeing you again, so I left Monday morning. Every little minute counted with me, and I wanted to spend all of them with you.

It may be a long time before I see you again, but remember, Margaret, I'll always love you. So don't worry and take care of yourself for me. I'll be back to you. Just love me as you have in the past, and the future will come out OK.

Bye now my darling.

Elijah Porter
10

---

[10] When Elijah and Margaret started to date, he wanted to take her out for Chinese food, and she refused. She would not eat it because her parents wouldn't eat it. During the 50s, there were rumors that Chinese people made their food with cats. At sixteen years old, she still wouldn't do anything like that if her parents wouldn't. After being employed on a job that they celebrated everyone in the office a birthday by ordering in Chinese food and a birthday cake she could not very well say no. So when it was her birthday, she got her first taste of Chinese food, which was pepper steak and rice. After that, she tasted more food and enjoyed it.

July 25, 1954

Dearest Darling,

You sure surprised me this time. But I like your surprises.

That was a very short visit I spent. You must have enjoyed it as much as I did because you seemed happy when I left.

The reception will be very nice. When everything is over and done with, then you will be happy and can relax for a while. To me, it doesn't mean too much, but if that is what you want, OK. Anything as long as you are happy, and I know this will make you happy because you have waited and hoped for this a long time. So I am praying that this will come out alright. I for one will be glad when this all over.

If I don't help you, you would be unhappy about the whole thing. After all, it is for both of us. So why can't I help you out? You don't have much money, and when I have some, I don't mind helping you. And you are not going too fast as next year is just around the corner. Before you know it, July will be here. If you weren't doing all those things, they wouldn't get done. I am away all the time and couldn't have half of them done by next year.

The Bedroom Suite and the Pots & Pans should be paid for. If not, I can pay the balance off when I get out. It will not be much, and I could pay it off without going into a hole.

The bus came about half an hour after you left, and I got back here that night. I bet you thought I wasn't going to kiss you when you had to leave. You should know better than that. I sure hated to see you go; you had to, and that is the trouble. We always have to leave each other. One day, this will be over, and all these goodbyes will be over.

Until then, be sweet and take care of yourself for me. I'll be back to you and remember I love only you. So long for now.

Yours always,
Elijah Porter

August 6, 1954

Dearest Darling,

Your letters were received yesterday, and they found me well.

Don't worry about the money for the things; we'll manage somehow whenever you send me the money. I'll take care of everything, but you don't have to worry about it. The bills will go down slowly, but for sure, they will go down. I am glad that you are willing to help me and not just helping me because I asked you.

I am looking around now for a band. I have one band in mind, but I am not sure of him yet. I will have to think about it for a while since he wants $160.00. Whatever I decide to do, I'll let you know.

By the way, can you paint maybe when I find the apartment? I'll let you come home to paint it (smile).

I am going to the store to pay on the furniture. Catherine is going with me so that I can show her the Bedroom Suite if it is still there.

Closing now.

Your sweetest little girl,
Margaret

August 17, 1954

Dearest Darling,

Last night, I almost didn't get a chance to talk to you when I called. Your Father told me that you were attending a club meeting, only he didn't say that you were next door until I was about to hang up, and then he called you to the telephone. I would have called you back tonight. You tried to kill yourself by running up the stairs. I could hear you running. Then when you got on the phone, you were all out of breath. It wasn't that important, and you didn't even have to come to the phone. I wouldn't have cared (smile).

There were a lot of things I wanted to talk to you about but didn't. They were not too important. I just wanted to hear your voice again; that was all. And a little while was better than not hearing you at all. If we had talked any more, your father would have to add a few more coins on his bill. I had seventy-five cents left after I finished. I could have sent you that six dollars, but I wanted to call you so I did. I got $1.75 until next payday. Then after that, I will be real broke for a while.

Well, so long for now, honey. I love you in my crazy way.

Yours,
Elijah Porter

August 23, 1954

Dearest Darling,

I received the money alright, just as you had sent it. I paid on the Pots & Pans, and I am going to save the rest toward the furniture.

Your voice was just as much appreciated as mine was to you. I am always glad to hear from you and especially to talk to you.

That letter that you sent to my mother, she received it but didn't say anything because I told her that I had changed my mind about going to visit you. When you stop to figure it out, we would spend about $50.00 to $60.00 for one day, and look what we could do with that money. I think we would be spending money foolishly, and we really can't afford it.

Write and let me know what you think of it. If you really want me to come, I'll come. I know that it would be alright with my mother and my father.

My mother and I are giving Catherine a surprise birthday party on Saturday, September 11th. Think that maybe you can make it?

Love,
Margaret
11

---

[11] Margaret and Elijah had been engaged for two years, and Margaret is now twenty years old. So her parents were OK with Margaret if she wanted to visit Elijah.

August 30, 1954

Dearest Darling,

Sometimes, a person can get very lonely being away from another person. They can't stand it at times, but they get over it. It just comes in spells. I know you have felt this way yourself, and somehow, you make it easier.

Yesterday, a fellow on this ship gave a bus ride to Bay Shore Beach. He asked me if I would come along. I told him no for a couple of weeks, but he talked me into going. Well, I went. The tickets for everything was $2.50, food and soda included.

They all had their wives and girls along, but you know something, I felt like a man from Mars. After we got there and I could go swimming, it didn't bother me. On the way back, it was about 2100. I really began to feel bad. My head was hurting, and my stomach was killing me, but that was my own fault. They had plenty of food; only I didn't eat. The chicken wasn't cooked the right way; it was boiled, and I didn't want to pull the skin off while all the people was around. And I don't eat anyone's half-boiled eggs, so I just didn't eat.

I tried to get away and relax some, but it did more wrong than good. I didn't enjoy myself at all. It is funny I can miss you so much like that. What is it that you do to me? I can't explain it, but it really is something that makes me feel funny inside. It will be a long time before I go out like that again. If I go out again, I will go over to the enlisted-men beach. It is just over the bay and don't cost any money to go there.

Well, anyway, Margaret, I thought I would tell you this so that you would see how I feel about you and how much I want to get out of here. I can't wait for next year to come. Only it isn't coming fast enough.

Until then, I'll try to take this as long as you are sweet and happy. I will be OK, just keep loving me like you do.

Yours,
Elijah Porter
12

---

12 Elijah is a very picky eater. He likes all of his food well done. That is why he would not eat then, and he will not eat now if the food is not well done

September 20, 1954

Dearest Darling,

While sitting down at work, with a few minutes to spare, I decided to drop you a few lines. I am fine, and I hope when you receive this letter, that you will be fine also.

I have been looking around for a band to play for the wedding reception.

My mother, father, Catherine, Mrs. Hattie and Mr. Otis and my cousin Jonnie B and I went to Keyport, New Jersey, to hear a band play that I had called; and he told me to come there in order that I may know what kind of music that he played. When I had called, he had told me that I would have to pay $160.00. When I talked to him on Saturday night in person, he said it would cost two hundred dollars. We think he jumped up his price because he saw all of the people that I was with. Anyway, I told him that he had said $160.00 before, so he went back to that amount. He also said that he couldn't promise me definitely that his band would play because they were looking for a summer job away from home for the entire summer, and that he couldn't let me know until May. He also said that if he couldn't play himself that he would find me someone else to play.

I also have another band to go and hear on October 9th at the Flamingo Room on Springfield Avenue in Newark. He wants $75.00. I'll have to see what happens, and I'll let you know.

By the way are you planning on coming home soon? I am going to a wedding on Sunday October 3rd. I was going to ask you to come home and go with me, but I changed my mind because none of the other girls is not bringing anyone; so I thought that you wouldn't want to be the only male with a table full of girls. It is Joan's wedding, the girl that works in the office with me. Please let me know what you think.

That is all for this time. I can't wait until July 23, 1955.

Write soon.

All my love to you,

Margaret

October 12, 1954

Dearest Darling,

By now, you must be wondering why you haven't received an answer from your last letter. Since I came back, you only got two letters; that was three weeks ago. The only trouble is we are a lot like each other sometimes. But you are the one that is getting very nervous and excited. I noticed that the last time, it won't be long, but it will be next year. I want this all to end too. Then neither of us will have to write these letters, and after all, talking to you in person would be nicer.

When we were down south the first of the year, I took some snapshots. It has been a long time, but I just got them printed. Some of them are of New York and New Jersey. You can tell which is which if you see a real handsome fellow on some of the pictures.

By now, you must know how much you mean to me, but every time I have to leave you, something happens to me. It took me longer to get straightened out this time than all the other times put together. Maybe it is because I enjoyed myself, or because I am looking forward to next year. I hate to leave you; I always think it is for good, only I hope that day will never come. I want to marry you more than anything else. If I can't love you and marry you at the same time, there wouldn't be anything left for me. But with you, I would be happy. I may not make a lot of money, but a small amount would be OK as long as you are happy, and you and I are happy together. That is all that matters with me.

To tell you the truth, I never thought that you would ever marry me. When I first came in here, I didn't think you would wait this long. I just knew you wouldn't, but that is how wrong a person can be about another person. Now you are still waiting, and I sure wouldn't like to go through this all over again. It would be too much for you and for me anyway. It is almost over, and we don't have much more time to remember those lonely nights that we spent apart.

It is getting time for me to close this letter before you have to pay for this letter, and that wouldn't be right after all. I am not that broke, or am I? I do have a few coins until Friday.

Well, so long for now and give everyone my regards, and be sweet for me. I love you even if I don't write to you regularly anymore.

Yours always,
Elijah Porter

October 17, 1954

Dearest Darling,

Last week, you wrote me a very nice letter. I wanted to answer Friday, when we got paid, but got lazy. Now here it is, Sunday, and just writing now. Don't you think that I am a stinker? (smile)

Every time I come home, even if it is for a short time, the last time wasn't any different. You make me happy by just seeing you only for a little while. I feel the same way as you do about me, and one day, we will be happy and won't have to do all of this.

I don't worry about you taking care of the money. I send to you, it means a lot to you and I know you will take care of everything.

Right now, I will not say anything about Ralph. When I see you again, I will. It wouldn't be right, and what is wrong, I'll tell you later.

Here is some more money for you, only I wish that it was a check for six hundred dollars.

Well, so long for now, honey. I still love you, Baby, even if you won't gain any weight (smile).

Yours,
Elijah Porter
13

---

[13] Elijah's mother and Margaret were going to the doctor, as his mother wanted to lose some weight and Margaret wanted to gain some. They did just the opposite of each other. His mother was gaining more weight, and Margaret was losing more weight. That is why she was being teased about not gaining any weight.

October 22, 1954

Dearest Darling,

I received your letters this week and also the money. Your letters found me well, and I hope that when you receive this letter that you will be fine also.

Don't worry about the other money that I had mentioned to you for the photographer. I will take care of it, so you don't have to borrow any money.

Jenell is very angry with me for buying so many things. She said that people will be very angry with me to when it comes to the shower and wedding gifts. I am not trying to do that, but I know better than anyone else what I need and want, so I have been buying them; but I am not going to buy anything else until after we are married.

Why won't you discuss Ralph and his awful doings. Are you afraid then he won't like you anymore? I am only teasing you.

By the way, my father got a brand new car this week. It is a 1954 Buick, very pretty. He was going to wait and to get a 1955, but he got the 1954 and saved $800.00.

You had better brush up on your driving because I am going to learn how to drive, and you wouldn't want me to be a better driver than you.

Looking forward to hearing from you soon. Everyone sends their love to you, and we are all counting down the time to July 23, 1955. The time is getting shorter and shorter, which is a good thing.

Yours always and with love,
Margaret
14

---

[14] Margaret's father just bought a brand new 1954 Buick. He decided that he would teach her how to drive. Number one, you should never take other people in the car with you when you are teaching someone to drive. Margaret's mother and sister were in the back seat of the car; her father and she were in the front when he

November 10, 1954

Dearest Darling,

Since I had some spare time here at the office, I decided that I would use it by dropping you this letter. You always say that I don't write you anymore. I am fine and hope that when you receive this letter, that you will be fine also.

The weather here is quite cold, but it isn't raining or snowing. I got a letter from my cousin Ruth in New York, and she said that it was raining and snowing there, so you see we are quite lucky.

Will you be home for New Year's Eve this year or not? I am planning to get all of the girls and boys together so that we can find out who can be in the wedding party.

I went to New York with some girls last Saturday night, and we saw *Carmen Jones*. the all-colored picture with Dorothy Danridge and Harry Belafonte. It was very good. Pearl Bailey also played in it.

I am very disappointed on my job. They are laying off people left and right in both the offices and in the factory. I don't think that I have to worry about being laid off; that is, not yet anyway. The only thing is that I am not making any overtime, and that is what I had

---

told her to make a right turn. And instead of putting her foot on the brake, she put her foot on the gas pedal and was going so fast that she was headed straight into a brick building. Margaret's father was having a hard time pulling us away from the building as he had lost his right hand at work many years ago and could only use one hand. Her sister was screaming so loud that she made Margaret even more nervous. When her father was able to help her stop the car, they had driven so far that she tore up a tire on his brand new car. It also cost her $200.00 to buy a new tire.

So much for Margaret, telling Elijah that she was going to be a better driver than him. That was in 1954, and she never tried again until 1958 and got her driver license. Margaret I'm happy to say that she have a good driving record of fifty-seven years as she have only gotten two speeding tickets and never had a car accident. She's praying that this record continues as she is eighty-one years old and still doing a little bit of driving. Elijah has had some accidents, but he was a very good driver, better than Margaret. "Was" because he has slowed down and don't do much highway driving anymore.

planned on to help buy some of the furniture with. But I won't be able to count on it any longer. At this rate, we won't be able to buy all of our furniture with cash as I had hoped. But we will have to do the best that we can.

Last year, I made from fifteen to twenty dollars a week in overtime around this time of the year, so you see that would have added up.

Are you going to help Issy in the store when you get out; that is, until we get married? Or are you going to wait until after we are married before you do anything about finding a job. It doesn't really make any difference to me. I was only wondering what you were going to do.

Elijah, I love you very much, and I want you all to myself and not sharing you or anything connected with you to anyone else to a certain extent. You can always help your family, but remember we come first with each other before anyone else. If I am wrong to feel this way, then I am really sorry, but that is the way that I love you and want you.

I hope when we get married that we will be very happy together. That is why I am trying to get everything straightened out now so that we will be happily married.

Love you,
Margaret

Planning the Wedding (Picture)

This picture was taken on February 7, 1955, when Elijah was home on leave. Margaret was ready to plan their wedding to be held on July 23, 1955.

Left to Right: Elijah in His Navy Uniform, Catherine Williams (Sister to Margaret), Margaret Williams, Iona Morrison (Sister to Elijah), Muriel Ware (Our Friend and Wife to Governor Ware), and Governor Ware (Our Friend).

Letters (1955)

Dearest Darling,

Just a few lines to let you know that I can still write. I know that you have forgotten that you have a girlfriend, when you look at the few letters that she has written to you.

I am fine and hope when you receive this letter that you will be fine also. Your visit home was enjoyed very much, but I hate weekends because they go too fast. Anyway, the little time that we do have together, I enjoy it.

Elijah, the way that I figure it, we aren't going to have enough money to pay cash for all of our furniture, so we'll just have to do the best that we can.

Do you know that we have spent at least $400.00 a piece for the wedding, furniture and other things already? And we still have a long way to go. We have to think about two month's rent for an apartment. We won't be home from our honeymoon until July 31st, and at that time, rent will be due again for August.

I figure that I'll have $1500.00 dollars in July, but most of my money will go for the wedding and reception. I'll only have money to buy all of the little things we need, like curtains, venetian blind spreads, pillows and a million other things that I could name. The kitchen set that I looked at cost $139.00. Since we are working toward our goal, I am sure that everything is going to be fine.

Your darling,
Margaret

March 1, 1955

Dearest Darling:

You are always giving me a hard time for not telling you anything. Well, now I will. It may not be what you would like, but you will know a little more.

A few months ago, I told you this ship was going out of commission. When we leave Philadelphia, we'll be up there from the 4th of April until the 4th of June. From there, it is going to Green Coves Springs, Florida. I thought that I would be getting out from here, but now it looks like I won't. As soon as we get to Florida, I'll leave for my discharge over in Jacksonville, Florida. So I won't be around New Jersey in June. I tried to get a transfer off here, but since my time is short, they will not put me on another ship; so maybe I'll get a chance to see my home again before I get too old (smile).

The weekend of February 26th, I'll be up there to see you. It means a lot to be with you on that day; the next one will not be like this one.

You are planning everything right now for July, so if you need me home for anything, let me know before the last of May. I can't get a lot of leave, but a few days will be OK, and if you find an apartment, don't worry about having it fixed up before I get out. I can help you, and we can have it real nice before July; you have enough to do now. Maybe I can come home often from Philadelphia if I can, then we can plan things out more. While I am there, I'll give you some money for other things, then you will have it if I cannot be on hand. Stop worrying so much; you want to do everything by yourself, and I feel left out in the cold.

You asked to buy the things for the ushers; save your money, that is my job. And Margaret, save something for me to do. I have three weeks before we get married, and I can be doing something in that time.

You are real sweet, but at times, you get too sweet and want to do everything. Then the first thing you know, you are tired and run down. Then when we get married, you won't be ready for the nights (smile).

Margaret, I love you very much and want July to come as much as you do, but it won't come any faster by us worrying our heads off. I wished it would though. I feel awful sometimes, and I know you must do too. Only don't stop telling me you love me, and then July will come soon. Until then, I can only hope and pray that I can be as good a husband as you said I have been as a boyfriend.

My love always,
Elijah Porter

March 3, 1955

Dearest Darling,

Since I was up there last week, I was not expecting any mail from you until next month, but I was wrong. A little seagull delivered me one today. It was real nice to hear from you so soon.

Margaret, about the money we will be needing, I know we will not have enough to buy all the things we will need. There are some things I can do without until we get all straightened out, and we still will be needing money all along. But you must remember we have more now than a lot of people have when they marry, only most of those people had it hard when they first started off.

In your next letter, try to find out how much all the other things will cost. Without the little things, I'll have $1,500.00 to spend on all the furniture. The other, I'll buy some of my clothing and pay for our honeymoon. We will have enough money to pay for the rent. I get a hundred dollars in July and August but that will not be nothing for us to use; it will all go into the bank or something else.

I understand how you feel about everything. I told you I want to buy a house for your next birthday, and if we don't have so many bills that will be that much more money, we will have saved up; and I really want a house for you as you deserve all of it and more, only I can't give you all of it now. All I worry about is getting a job when I get out of here. Any kind of job is alright as long as I can make some money, not a whole lot but enough for you and I to live on.

Well, so long for now and take it easy. I'll have enough to pay off most of the furniture, if not all of it. Everything is going to work out.

Bye now and be sweet.

Yours,
Elijah Porter
[15]

---

[15] This letter was written March 3, 1955. We got married July 23, 1955. Bought our house April 1957, a little less than two years after we got married.

May 27, 1955

Dearest Darling,

Before I came down here to Florida, I was going to write you mostly all the time; but after getting here, things have changed. You wrote me about two weeks ago, and I am just now answering it. See what kind of husband you are getting; maybe you better get rid of him before you regret it. I hope you will never regret waiting for me this long and still not complain. Most grown up little ladies would have given up a long time ago even before I asked you to marry me. So you see I have a reason for wanting to get back there to you. You are one girl in a million, and don't think that I don't know it.

I love you and want to leave this place right now, but the man say I have to stay until my time is up in this outfit. It will not be long now, but I wonder if I can hold out that long the way I feel now. I haven't seen any of my folks here in Florida yet, and I may not; I just want to leave.

I get out the Friday of the 23rd of June. You may get a telegram from me that night, so don't get all upset. I will be sending you some money to hold for me until I get there. It will be too much for me to carry around in my pocket, and you have a checking account, so why not put it in the bank. So when you need the money, you will have it even if all the banks are closed. Oh yes, you are telling me how to buy clothing for myself. Well, you are going with me to pick out some of them. Then if you don't like what I am wearing, you will have no one to fault but yourself. Maybe that will keep you quiet for a while. But knowing you, that will only make you want to go that much more. I will only let you pick out some, not all of them. I still like dungaree even if you are going to kill me later. It will not be long because I will have five suits if my shopping is left up to you (smile).

I am going to buy Mrs. Hattie and your mother a gift while I am down here, but I am wondering when to give it to them, maybe before the wedding or when I come home. They will still get something from me. And don't think I have forgotten your father and your sister since I have been in service. I have only given them one present that is awful after looking at all the things you have given to my family. I have a lot of things to make up with not only with them but to you also.

I love you very much and want to be with you all the time. Our time has been spent rushing so much that I didn't appreciate your good nature.

Love you,
Elijah Porter
16

---

[16] Elijah wore Navy uniforms the entire time that he was in the service, so he had no other clothes.

Wedding Invitation

Mr. and Mrs. Claude Williams

request the honour of your presence

at the marriage of their daughter

Margaret

to

Elijah Porter

son of Mr. and Mrs. Samuel Porter

on Saturday, the twenty-third of July

Nineteen hundred and fifty-five

at four o'clock

Mount Calvary Baptist Church

242-244 Prince Street

Newark, New Jersey

Reception five-thirty o'clock

at Wideway Ballroom, 929 Broad Street

Newark, New Jersey

Wedding Day

At last, our wedding day is here after dating and planning for this day for five years.

Even though we planned and prepared for this day, we found that we still could use some help in making it a dream wedding.

My godmother Hattie Hopkins brought me the most beautiful wedding gown that anyone could imagine.

A family friend, Maggie Floyd, paid for the wedding cake that Elijah and I could not have afforded, as she thought the cake that I wanted was much too small. She chose the one that she thought was right for us.

My parents helped with the reception. Our budget had not planned for such expensive items as these, and we were eternally grateful.

Wedding Pictures

Margaret with Her Parents

Margaret with Her Bridal Party

Margaret, Elijah, Margaret's Godparents, and a Very Dear Friend

Margaret and Elijah with Their Parents

Elijah and Margaret Cutting the Wedding Cake

Margaret and Elijah with Margaret's Grandmother

Elijah and Margaret's Honeymoon in Atlantic City, New Jersey

Elijah and Margaret's First Apartment (Picture)

They took this picture after they came home from church.

Family

When Elijah and Margaret got married after dating for five years and had never been intimate, their life was far more than they had ever thought about in their wildest dreams. They could be with each other in every way, and they did since they did not have a television until five months after they got married.

We were married for seven years before deciding to have a family. We wanted to build our life together and just enjoy being married, and that is what we did. Many people tried to push us into starting a family, but we were in charge, just as we always were; and we did what we wanted on our terms and no one else.

In 1962, I became pregnant but miscarried within a few months so early that we never knew what the sex of the baby would have been.

On February 8, 1964, on Margaret's birthday, she gave birth to a beautiful baby boy named Mark Ira. All during Margaret's pregnancy, Elijah was hoping for a daughter first.

In 1964, you could not determine the sex of an unborn child. It would have been great for me. I told Elijah that since he wanted a daughter so badly, it would not happen. I could not understand why he would want a girl around since when he was still at his home, he had seven sisters. Although it was not a girl first, we were very happy with our son Mark.

In 1966, Elijah's dream did come true when a beautiful baby girl was born, named Elana Victoria.

Mark joined the Navy, following his father's footsteps. After boot camp, he was stationed in Italy, and there he met Rosella Maria Cananta (Rosie). They were married in 1985, and in 1987, our beautiful granddaughter, Alicia Marie, was born. She was born in Belleville, New Jersey, with Elijah and I since Mark was away on the Navy for a six-month tour duty. He never saw Alicia until she was six months old.

Elana never married, and in 2001, we lost her to a drive-by shooting that struck and killed her. She was in her car, in the wrong place, at the wrong time as she did not know the person or anyone involved with the shooting.

Family Pictures

Margaret with Their Children

Elana and Elijah
Mark in High School and Navy

Mark and Rosie's Wedding
Elana as Maid of Honor, Eddie as Best Man

Left: Mark

Margaret, Elijah with Their Children

Top Left: Elijah, Rosie, Alicia, Margaret, and Mark
Top Right: Rosie and Alicia
Bottom Left: Margaret, Elijah, and Alicia
Bottom Right: Elijah, Alicia, and Margaret

Margaret and Elijah's Granddaughter, Alicia

This picture was taken when Elijah and Margaret became grandparents to their granddaughter, Alicia Marie Porter, born April 20, 1987. We were still smiling three months later.

Alicia, Elijah, and Mark

Closeness of Elijah and Margaret

Just how close Elijah and Margaret were, and still are today, when Margaret needed to speak to him for whatever reason, he would feel the need to call her in order to do this. He first had to find a public telephone booth. This book is set in 1955, before anyone had cell phones.

After Elijah and Margaret were married, one Saturday morning, he decided to go out with his brother-in-laws and other friends to play basketball, which he loved. When he left, Margaret was home, and she was in the midst of doing their laundry by hand as they did not have a washing machine. After washing all of the clothes, they had to be hung outside on a clothesline to dry.

Since it was in August, and a very hot summer day, Margaret was in her nightgown and alone in the house. She felt that going out to the back porch to hang the clothes in her nightgown would be alright, how wrong she was as the landlord who lived on the first floor had a big black dog that came upstairs to the second floor where she was hanging out the clothes. Margaret did not want the dog to go into her apartment, so she closed the door to keep him out. Not only did she keep the dog out but she also kept herself out since closing the door. It locked without a key.

Elijah, after playing basketball for a while, being a newly married man, he decided to call home to see if Margaret was all right. She was home on the back porch in her nightgown and could hear the telephone ringing, but she could not answer it. Margaret had not told him that she would be going out, so he right away felt that something was not right. He told his brother-in-laws that he had to go home so that he could check on Margaret. Of course they laughed and thought, "Here we go. This man could not be away from his wife for five minutes." They took him home to see about Margaret, only to find her locked out on the back porch. He let her into the apartment. She was happy to see him, and at that moment she knew that whenever she would need him, he would be there.

There were many times that Elijah would find a telephone to call Margaret to talk to her or just to hear her voice for a minute.

In 1987, Margaret had gone to San Diego California with Rosie, her daughter-in-law, and her granddaughter Alicia to meet Mark who was coming home on the ship from his six-month tour in the navy. Rosie had stayed in New Jersey with Elijah and Margaret so that Alicia could be born near them and not in San Diego by herself. This was going to be the first time that Mark would see his beautiful baby girl.

Margaret only wished that she had taken some pictures of this event as it was something that she will always remember, seeing the ship dock with all of the new fathers standing on one deck to get off first to see all of their new babies that were born while they were away. It was one of the most beautiful sights that she had ever seen. Mark holding Alicia for the first time was great to watch. They even made the six o'clock news on television.

Margaret, Rosie, and Alicia were staying with friends of Rosie and Mark while waiting for the ship to arrive, and Margaret wanted to talk to Elijah but could not call him in New Jersey on someone else's telephone. However, at six in the next morning, the telephone rang; and the owner of the house said that the call was for Margaret. She was not too happy for her telephone to ring at six in the morning, and she told Margaret so. Elijah said that he could not wait any later as he knew that they needed to talk to each other, and it was 9:00 a.m. in New Jersey. Elijah had come thru for Margaret. Again, no cell phones.

Another time, Margaret needed Elijah when she was giving her supervisor a ride home after they were done at work. It was pouring rain, and Margaret's car cut off at the end of Ravine Place in Nutley, the road that she was driving on to take her home. After the car would not start, again, she went to find a telephone booth to call home to see if Elijah had gotten home from work and could come to help them. He was not home, so she left a message on the answering machine. Within fifteen minutes at the most, Elijah drove up in the back of Margaret's car, not knowing that she was there. He would not take that road home at any other time, and somehow, he did that day. They asked him if had he gotten the message Margaret left on the answering machine, and he said no as he had just gotten off the Garden State Parkway and was heading home. Here again, he knew when Margaret needed him.

How can you not say that Margaret and Elijah have a great love connection between them? And Margaret is sure that it was guided also by their love of God.

Special Card to Elijah

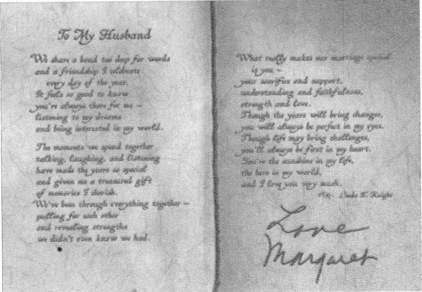

Travels

When I met Elijah and fell in love with him, I had no idea that I would travel and see some of the places that he had seen while he was in the military.

All of these travels were made possible when we joined a reunion group from the first ship that he was on—USS Belle Grove LSD.

These are some of the places that we have traveled: Columbus, Ohio; Orlando, Florida; Des Moines, Iowa; Portsmouth, Virginia (where Elijah and I were the hosts along with Del, Catron, Ike, and Alice Tanis); Springfield, Missouri; San Diego, California; Houston, Texas; Newport, Rhode Island; Las Vegas, Nevada; Omaha, Nebraska; Lafayette, Louisiana; Settle, Washington. We had a cruise to Alaska; Denver, Colorado; Kerrville, Texas; Philadelphia, Pennsylvania; Branson, Missouri; Albuquerque, New Mexico; Appleton, Wisconsin; and Maryland/Washington, DC.

I may have missed a few. These are the ones that I remember as these trips started in 1991. The reunion group is still together, and we are looking forward to traveling to Dallas, Texas in July 2017

Another example of what Elijah would do for me was to always, as he would say in his letters, love me. In 1998, two weeks before we were to leave to go to Texas for a navy reunion, I fell and broke my right ankle and my right arm at the same time. Elijah said that we could not attend the reunion even though everything was paid for—airline tickets, tours, etc.

He said that I would be in too much pain and shouldn't be away from home and my doctor. However, I didn't want to hear any of this, insisting that I would be in pain no matter where I was, at home or in Texas.

After speaking to our dear friends Ike and Alice, whom we always traveled to the reunions with, they insisted that we still go to the reunion. I borrowed a wheel chair from a friend, and off we all went to Texas with leg in a cast and arm in a sling. I had the time of my life at the reunion as everyone there was happy to see me and took care of me. I had very little pain as Elijah would put ice packs and wrap my leg the same way at night that they had done for me in the hospital.

Girls, when you find the right man for you—and I did—you can trust that he did mean every word that he had said in those letters that he had written to me and proved it over and over to me.

Margaret and Elijah Porter's Golden Wedding Anniversary

July 23, 1955 to July 23, 2005
The Bethwood,
38 Lackawanna Avenue,
Totowa, New Jersey

Margaret and Elijah's Golden Wedding Anniversary
Elijah did not want to renew their wedding vows.
A vow that was written by Margaret was read at the party.
It reflected their fifty years of marriage called Our Love.

Our Love

Margaret and Elijah met when she was fifteen. Elijah was invited to her sixteenth birthday party. They started to date after her party. On February 26, 1950, Elijah came to Margaret's home and asked her if she had a boyfriend, and she said no. Elijah said, "Would you like one?" And she said yes.

They had many dates until 1951, when Elijah decided to go into the navy for four years. Margaret said that she had to be in love with him to wait four years, as they were the longest four years of her life.

Our other friends went into the army for two years, and Elijah was still serving his time. We didn't see each other often because he was at sea. The time that we did spend together was quality time.

Our faith in God has brought us through everything that life has dealt us, the good and the bad, but most of all, each other. During our fifty years of marriage, we were blessed with two children and one granddaughter, and many wonderful family and friends.

The most important thing in a marriage is that you both have the same core values and then you know that together, you can accomplish anything with the help of God.

Small things are just as important as big things, such as saying thank you and please. We say this to each other all the time. Helping each other do whatever needs to be done, whether it is cooking, washing dishes, taking out the garbage, or doing the laundry. When you are a couple, everything that needs to be done, you're both responsible for it. When you can say that you can do all of these things, then you know that you want to spend the rest of your life with each other.

Elijah and Margaret have such a strong bond to each other that Elijah knows when Margaret needs him without her calling him. It is not easy to find your soul mate, but you know that you have when you love each other, yell at each other, laugh and cry with each other, and finish each other's sentences or think about the same things at the same time.

It is said, "In a marriage, you should become one." We have truly, in our fifty years, became one.

Special Pictures

Mark Alicia Rosie Margaret Elijah

Margaret Elijah

Margaret and Mark

Top: Elijah and coworkers from his job. He retired after forty years.
Bottom: Margaret's coworkers from her job. She retired after seventeen years.

Elijah and Margaret's Friends from the USS Belle Grove Reunion Group

Family and Friends

Margaret and Elijah with Family

Family and Friends

**Margaret and Elijah's Church Family at Mount Calvary Baptist Church
Newark, New Jersey
Rev. Ralph M. Branch (Pastor)**

Margaret and Elijah Cutting Cake at Fiftieth Anniversary Party

Family and Friends

Mother's Day Story

One day, I heard a story about a woman that was complaining about her husband that he never gave her a gift on Mother's Day, and she was the mother of their two children. He said that she was not his mother.

Elijah and I have been married for sixty years, and he has said the exact same thing. That the reason that he doesn't give me a Mother's Day gift is because I am not his mother.

His gift to me as a wife and mother is how he treats me all year long, and that is like a queen.

I do have a funny story to tell about Elijah taking me out for dinner on Mother's Day, which he always did before and after we had children.

One year, he did not make a reservation for dinner at any restaurant, and everyone knows that Mother's Day is the busiest day of the year.

We went to one restaurant in Belleville, New Jersey as Elijah knew the owners and thought that maybe we could get a last minute reservation, and we could not. The owners said that we could sit at the bar and enjoy some of the finger foods served before dinner. We did, but since it was only finger foods, we still wanted dinner.

In a restaurant in Rutherford, New Jersey, there we found that we could have dinner without a reservation; so we ended up with a full-course dinner. I had never eaten so much food as I am a small eater, and my stomach was too full.

As soon as we got outside to the car, I threw up everything that I had eaten. I was not drunk as I had not had any alcohol, only food. This was how I paid my loving husband for taking me out to dinner instead of buying me a gift.

Special Awards from Church

Margaret and Elijah were married at Mount Calvary Baptist Church Newark, New Jersey, in 1955.

In 2006, when this award was given, it was in honor to Margaret and Elijah as they were the only couple still members of the church, married there, and both spouses still alive and have celebrated more than fifty years of marriage.

Margaret and Elijah on their Wedding Day
July 23, 1955

Margaret and Elijah on their Fiftieth Anniversary
July 23, 2005

Words of Congratulations

*Marriage is sharing
as husband and wife
The magic and meaning
love brings to your life.
It's laughing about
funny moments you've known.
And looking back fondly
on ways you've both grown...*

*It's being a couple
and also best friends,
Together in solving
the problems life sends.
It's loving each other
in all that you do.
With a bond that grows sweeter
your whole lifetime through.*

*Wishing you an anniversary
as special
as the love you share.*

You are an inspiration
to me and a
whole lot of lessons to learn.
From. Maria C

You know we feel ♡
Bev

Happy 60th! Wow!!
John, Sabita & Steph

Love you,
love so much
Reggie

We love
you both so
much,
Michael & Brinda

Wow! 60!
Awesome! We
love you guys
Cell + Lou

Much Love
Angela
+
Jacob

Love you both
Robert + Wife

Happy Anniversary
to the best couple
seen!!!
Rich + Karen

God Bless
Michelle Andrew

With love
Jeannie

Praise the
Lord!
Mommy + Ess

God bless both
of you
Kim

God Bless
Congrad
Love Amon

Graceway Church

245

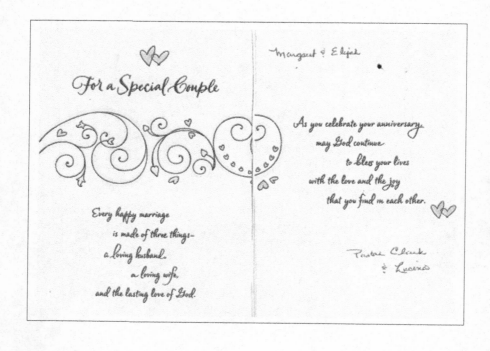

Sixtieth Wedding Anniversary

Special Pictures

Margaret, Earl, and Elijah

Margarite, Mark with white dog

Elaine and Carolyn

Carol and Dee Dee

Alicia and Mark

Margaret and Elijah's son, Mark, is famous for roasting a whole pig, which was on the menu at their sixtieth anniversary party.

Sixtieth Anniversary Party

Pam

David

Mark and Pam

Elijah and I were so very happy to see every one of our guest at our sixtieth anniversary party. However, the ones that touched our hearts the most are two in the pictures below. My cousin Carolyn wanted to come to our party so bad, but she lives in Chicago. Her daughter, realizing how close her mom and I have always been, decided to make it possible. Jackie lives in Atlanta, Georgia. She flew to Chicago to pick up her mom and then they flew in to Boston, rented a car, and drove to Middletown, Rhode Island so that they could be with us for our party. No family member could be loved more.

Married for Life

When Elijah and Margaret got married, they said that they would honor their vows and be married for life.

If a marriage is to last a lifetime, it requires the same level of energy and devotion from both of the partners. Each must give 100 percent, maybe not all at the same time, but it must be there.

They were always available to the other, fully present to listen and to talk.

"You only get out a marriage what you put into it. Having fun together, laughing whenever you can poke fun with each other. God gives to us richly all things to enjoy. Do everything you can to express your love to each other; we try to do this daily," Margaret said.

However, Elijah is not a person that likes to show his love by hugging and kissing in public but showing to Margaret in many other ways. He is still talking about Margaret just the same as he did when he was in the navy sixty-five years ago. Elijah talks about how happy he is to be married to Margaret and is very protective of her; he lets everyone know it.

Elijah likes to bring orange juice to Margaret early in the morning before making a big breakfast as Margaret is not an early breakfast person. Elijah's health is not as good as it could be, but Margaret encourage him to do what he can to keep himself busy and to not get bored. He has had a mild stroke and now has dementia and do not remember everything as well as he did in the past.

Elijah and Margaret have experienced a lot of problems throughout their lives, but they did not let anything defeat them. Every experience only drew them closer to each other.

Elijah and Margaret took one day at a time, and before they knew it, they had celebrated fifty years of marriage on July 23, 2005. They blinked and now have celebrated sixty years of marriage on July 23, 2015. Only thru the grace of God could all of these have happened.

Always love each other and share common goals. This explains why a man leaves his father and mother, and is joined to his wife; and the two are united into one.

Margaret was always treated like a lady should be, and when she felt that Elijah was not treating her the way that she wanted to be, he was called on it; and everything always turned out all right. Elijah learned that husbands should be considerate when you live with your wives and always treat them with respect. Love takes maintenance and kindness; be kind to one another.

Don't expect to have everything right from the beginning of your marriage. When Elijah and Margaret got married, Elijah had just gotten out of the navy on June 17, 1955, about a month before their wedding day on July 23, 1955. Elijah did not have a job as Margaret did not want him to find one until after the wedding so that they could have a honeymoon. Elijah and Margaret had found an apartment after he came home for good. Only they didn't have time to paint it before leaving on their honeymoon. Elijah's brother, Sherman, painted their apartment while they were gone, and when they returned, all that they had to do was have their furniture delivered as most of it had already been chosen and paid for with a very small balance due. Elijah did find a job after he and Margaret married and got back from their honeymoon. They finished paying for their furniture and saved money to buy their home on April 1957 with the help of family. It was a three-family house. They lived there for sixteen years, and their children, Mark and Elana, were born there. In today's world, I would not suggest that you get married to anyone that doesn't have a job.

In 1973, they moved to Nutley, New Jersey, so that their children could go to a better school than they would have while living in

Newark, New Jersey. In 1989, the complex that they had moved into in Nutley became a co-op apartment. They brought their apartment and lived in Nutley for thirty-nine and a half years before moving to Middletown, Rhode Island, in February 2013. They moved there to live with their son Mark as Elana is deceased and Mark wanted his parents to be closer to him.

Always be faithful and true to each other. Elijah ended up becoming a plumber. As you know that plumbers are alone in many women homes. Margaret was never jealous of him, as he never gave her a reason not to trust him.

"Over the years, we have many friends that love him for who he was and is still the same today. Elijah has always been quiet a person that liked to joke with everyone, including women," said Margaret.

Elijah and Margaret's faith and trust in God kept them true to their vows and faithfulness to each other. It is all right to agree or to disagree as long as you both know to be loving about it. If it is a bad argument, cool down as quickly as possible. This was always easier for Elijah for he never liked to argue and still don't. Margaret, on the other hand, could argue longer; but you can't argue by yourself. A fool gives full vent to his anger, but a wise man keep himself under control.

Never keep score on who did what; marriage is not a contest in which you and your spouse would want to keep score against each other. God has placed you on the same team so you can strive together toward your goals, to serve each other with love. You have to like each other in order to really communicate. Try your best to let God's spirit keep your hearts united. Elijah and Margaret kept their love, their health, and their faith in God strong.

You do not have to like everything; the same Elijah and Margaret do not have the same taste in food. Margaret pretty much like all kinds of food. She is only fussy when it comes to eating eggs. She likes them cooked all kind of ways as long as there are not any brown spots. Elijah likes all of his food well done. Also, Margaret likes coffee and Elijah doesn't, but he can make a good pot of coffee. He was a very good cook until they moved to Middletown, Rhode Island. The reason was that he was used to cooking on a gas burner stove, and now he is cooking on an electric stove and they are hard to adjust to. Spend as much time together; go out for breakfast, lunch, and dinner as often as you can.

Margaret feels lucky to be married to Elijah and that she could find a young man at the age of sixteen, dated for five years, married for sixty years, and he is still the joy of her life. They have loved, traveled, and enjoyed being married to each other. When you marry, remember that you are committing for a lifetime.

Words of Congratulations

To Aunt Margaret and Uncle Elijah,

Congrats on your 60th anniversary!
Love you both & wish you many more.

Andrew, Marie Johnson Daniels, Devin, and Christopher
***

I love you both.

From Lillie M. Hill, Ranzy Hill, Springfield Mass
***

You're an inspiration to so many. Happy Anniversary.

George Carter and Randle
Newport, RI
***

Your love is inspirational. Congrats on 60 years of marriage. May God bless the both of you with so many more.

With love,
Marie and Shawn
Newport, RI
***

What an example you two are. In love, life, and God. Clark and I will do our best to follow your lead. God bless you both.

Lucina
***

Praise God for an outstanding example of love and compassion for one another. May you have many more years.

Marlene
***

Congratulations!

Jackie Wright, Cousin
Atlanta

Carolyn Wright, Cousin
Chicago
***

May God continue to bless you.

David Brown
Connecticut
***

Aunt Margaret & Uncle Elijah,
It's amazing to see how God has continued to use and bless you! Your 60 years is a testimony to God's goodness. You are truly an inspiration to those around you. That laughter and a sincere heart can accomplished! You are a delight and a measure stick!

Love,
Andrea Y. Morrison
***

Dear Aunt Margaret & Uncle Elijah,

I wish you many more annaveristey to come. (Kennedy)
***

Dear Aunt Margaret & Uncle Elijah,
I wish you 60 more years of marriage and hope it last forever.

Love,
Madison
***

To my uncle and aunt,
God bless you both with many more years of happiness, health, laughter. Love you both.

Gerald Waltz
***

Cousin Elijah & Margaret,
Happy to be here & I enjoyed myself. Happy 60th Anniversary.
8/16/15
Carol B.
***

Happy Anniversary.

Love,
Kevin B
***

Cousin Elijah & Margaret,
Love! Love! Love!
Happy 60 and many, many more.

Love,
Cousin DeeDee & Nyia
***

Mrs. Margaret & Mr. Elijah,
Please know this is a wonderful occasion being I was a part of it.
Happy Anniversary in love to each other.

God bless,
Myrtle
***

Praise the Lord for his faithfulness to you both! God's love is reflected
through your marriage and contentment to the Lord and each other!
Thank you for letting us celebrate with you!

Manny and Elsie
***

It was a privilege to meet you both. Love and all my respect!

Maria & Marcos
***

God bless you both. You two have been married as long as I have
been on earth. So happy to have known both of you. Love you, and
I feel like both of you are my family.

Donna
***

Cousin Margaret & Elijah,
It is so nice to be here to celebrate your anniversary and meet family
and friends. This is a beautiful day. God bless you.

Love you,
Your Utica Family
Elaine B. Shaw
***

God bless you both. You are very important to me. Love you.

Kim Burke
***

Dearest Ms. Margaret & Elijah,
You are so very dear to us. May we remain good friends forever!
Happy 60th!

Love & God bless,
Michael & Linda Burns
***

Dear Margaret & Elijah,
I pray God blesses you with many more anniversaries. You are blessed
people & we love you.

Angela & Jacob Scott
***

We wish you many more.

Willie Moore & Cousin Mary Moore
***

Aunt Margaret & Uncle Elijah,
What a role model for love and devotion. Love you.

Toni
***

Congratulations! Many more years of happiness.

The Dugans
***

Congratulations!

Your cousin, Moses Hill
***

Margaret & Elijah,
May god bless you & watch over you!

Love,
xxoo Jeanne
***

Margaret & Elijah,
Happy Anniversary. May God watch over you & bless you always.

Love
Linda Desimone
***

Margaret & Elijah,
Happy Anniversary. Thank you for showing us what a good marriage
is. God bless you.

Love,
Beverly L. Franklin
***

Karen-Rick David—Happy Anniversary!!!
You two are an inspiration in so many ways!
***

Happy 60th Anniversary Margaret & Elijah! You are an inspiration to all your shipmates and friends. We wish you all the best with many years of wedded bliss.

Carol Sandrowski!
***

Dear Grandma and Grandpa,
You are such an inspiration for me. Your love, life and strength.
I wish you a very happy anniversary!!
I love you!

Alicia
***

Dear Mr. & Mrs. Porter,
Congratulations and Thank you for allowing me to be a part of your celebration. Your love and years together are truly inspiring to those of us who think we know what love & marriage are. God bless & many more years to come.

Love,
Gina
***

Mom & Dad,
When people think about your 60+ years together, they don't realize that it actually means 21, 915 days. By the way, out of all of those days, I have been a part of 18,315 of those wonderful days!!
Happy Anniversary!!

Love,
Mark

Final Thoughts
(Margaret)

When I was growing up as a teenager, I always loved myself, had great self-esteem, and was proud in knowing what I wanted out of life. I was never a follower, doing what all of my friends were doing. Today, I feel that girls think that in order to have a boyfriend, they have to follow the crowd to be liked. This is not true. If you talk to a group of your friends and you stick together to let boys know how you feel, things could change.

Boys, stop wanting to get girls to do what you want them to do. Remember one day, you are going to grow up to be young men ready for marriage, and the girls that you were having a good time with, or so you thought, will not be the girl that you want to marry. Also think that one day, you will be a father with a daughter, and fathers are the first ones to want to break some boy's neck for disrespecting their daughter. There is no greater love between parents and their children than between fathers and their daughters. Fathers love their sons, but daughters are different. Have you heard the expression "Daddy's little girl"? Well, this is true. No matter how old Daddy's little girl becomes, she is still the same to him.

Elijah was a navy man, and in the 1950s, navy men had a bad reputation. It was said that they had a girl in every port and that all they did was drink a lot of alcohol and have lots of sex. He traveled all over the world; how would I know what he was doing? He would tell me that he was not having sex with anyone, and he wouldn't if he could not have sex with me. There was no way that I could

273

know if this was true. I only had his word, which I choose to believe. However, if I was having sex in New Jersey while he was in the navy, traveling all over the world, he would know about it because men are just that way. They would be happy to tell everyone, including him, that they were having sex with me while he was away in the navy.

We did not talk about out our sex life with anyone as we thought that it was private between us and God. When you are dating and do not want to have sex until you both feel it is right, and your relationship is where you want it to be and neither of you would get hurt by it, then it is time to do it. Just make sure that you have the right person and not some sweet-talking guy who is only concerned for his needs. If you are in a relationship, especially teen-agers, there are going to be weak moments, but one person always has to be strong when the other person is weak; and together, you can wait until it is right. You can be loving together and in love with each other without sex.

Elijah and I grew up in the church, and we are sure that. We were aware of our Christian values. In reading the Bible now and reading different scriptures. I am sure that we learned to depend and trust in Jesus Christ without fully understanding why. The magic of first love is our believing that it can never end. Our relationship started February 26, 1950 and is still lasting strong for us to have celebrated sixty years of marriage on July 23, 2015.

Elijah and I want to thank God for the foresight of mind to keep all of the love letters that we wrote to each other more than sixty-five years ago. There were forty-eight months of letters that we had saved.

Our family and friends have been so supportive and encouraging while I wrote this book. Elijah and I have had an amazing journey with each other over these last sixty-five years. I say sixty-five years, as we dated for five years and have now celebrated sixty years of marriage.

It has been a happy time to remember the good and the bad times that we have shared. This book is not about our family and friends' lives, only the courtship, love, and marriage that was born out of our relationship with each other and the people who helped us on this journey.

We are not saying that we were perfect yesterday or today and have never made any mistakes along the way of our lives. Every human being on this earth has made mistakes, but we all know that these mistakes or sins, if you want to call them, has been forgiven by Jesus when He died on the cross for all of us.

Elijah and I have never condemned or judged young people or anyone as to how they went on their journey in their lives. We felt that our journey was different and did what was best for us.

I understand that the 1950s was a much different time than now, in 2015. People are still the same yesterday, today, and tomorrow. They all do the same things as they see fit. The big difference is in the '50s we had only peer pressure. When Elijah and I started to date, there were only two channels on the television from six o'clock in the morning until twelve in the morning, and there never was sex shown on the television like it is today. Couples on television could not sleep in the same bed together.

Today, there is so much more with all kinds of social media, Facebook, sex and more sex shown everywhere. Girls, I would advise you to stop taking pictures of yourselves for your boyfriends to see you without your clothes on. Any boy that asks you to do this does not have your best interest at heart. For if he did, then he would never ask you to do such a thing and then turn around and show your pictures to all of their friends or post them on Facebook. Girls, stay out of boys' bedrooms and keep them out of yours and never with the doors closed. Elijah and I were never in a room with closed doors in 1950s, and girls, you should not be in a room with closed doors in 2015. Parents, help your children with this. As long as parents say to them that it is all right, then they are going to do it.

When girls are in the habit of doing whatever boys ask them to do, you are giving them the wrong impression of you, and this is when they begin to disrespect you. You are lowering your self-esteem. Girls, always keep your self-esteem high as only you can do this.

Many people over the years have told us that they see the love between us. My cousin Emma said that I had found a winner in getting married to Elijah. Over the years, Emma gave us the names Elijah the King and Margaret the Queen. When she was asking me about Elijah, she'd say, "How is the king?" In Mount Calvary Baptist Church, Newark, New Jersey, where Elijah and I grew up and got married in, the members there referred to us as the lovebirds. We have also been called the lovebirds in our new church, Graceway Community Church, Middletown, Rhode Island. So no matter where we are, people can see that we love each other.

This book was geared mostly to teenagers. I hope that every teenager that reads this book will get something of value from it. I want all teenagers to have a good and happy life through their love with whomever they choose to marry, as Elijah and I did. It takes a lot of time, work, communication, and love for each other.

Intimacy is closeness, caring, tenderness, fondness, affection, warmth, camaraderie, and love making after marriage. You can feel all of these things without making love until you both are ready for it. Just make sure when you do that, you won't get hurt by it.

Teenagers should never have sex, as most of the time, it only causes heartache; and you have no idea how to handle it. Older women, you can make a different choice for yourselves, but you should follow the same rules. Don't jump; take your time as well.

My final thought is this. Girls or women, always insist that boys or men treat you with respect. Remember that we, as women, have all the power; and don't ever forget this no matter what you are told.

About the Author

Margaret was born in Blakely Georgia in 1934, her parents moved to New Jersey when she was an infant, so she grew up in New Jersey.

Margaret went to Grammar High School and Business Prep School in New Jersey. She always had many friends and still does dating back to her school, church and employment work places.

Her nice warm smile, the care she has for everything and everyone Margaret gets involved with and the integrity from within sums up to the amazing woman she is.